30 REAL SIGNS FROM THE AFTERLIFE

30 REAL SIGNS *from the* AFTERLIFE

RECOGNIZING *and* UNDERSTANDING MESSAGES *from* LOST LOVED ONES

MELISSA St. HILAIRE

callisto
publishing
an imprint of Sourcebooks

To my beloved friend, Amy Wallace, who left us too soon but still sends me signs from the afterlife nearly every day.

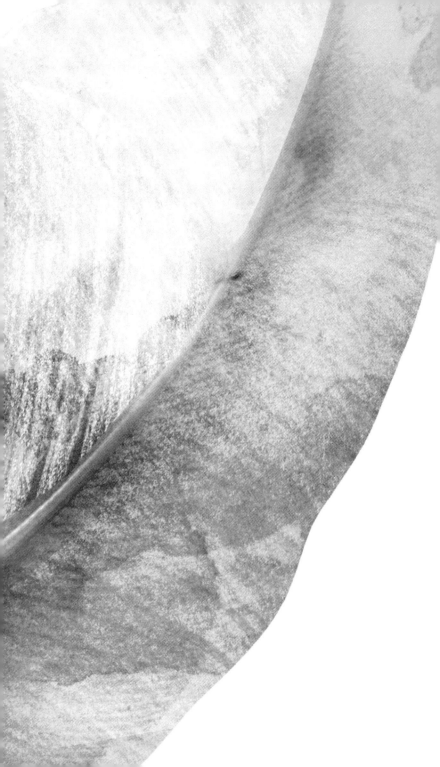

CONTENTS

INTRODUCTION

Welcome to *30 Real Signs from the Afterlife*! My name is Melissa St. Hilaire. I'm a professional psychic-medium, and I'm wicked passionate about this topic.

I grew up in rural Massachusetts, where my grandmother taught me how to see fairies and sense the spirits of people who lived on our land before us. But my experience with the afterlife really started when I was three years old. My grandfather had recently passed. I walked into my grandma's bedroom and asked, "Why are you crying?"

"Because Grandpa is gone," she replied.

"No, he isn't," I said. "He's over there." I pointed to a chair in the corner.

Ever since then, whenever I have traveled to historical locations, like Salem, Massachusetts, or famously haunted buildings, like the Winchester Mystery House in San Jose, California, I have had "strange" experiences. But I never took them seriously—not until one encounter.

Shortly after learning that one of my dearest friends had unexpectedly passed, I felt something odd. A hand touched my shoulder, but there was no one there. The air was full of static electricity, and I felt a breath on my ear.

I heard my friend's voice whisper, "It's okay, Melissa. I'm not in pain anymore."

I couldn't shake this experience. I'd felt energies and seen entities, but I had never before heard a voice so clearly from a dearly departed one. After hearing from my friend, I decided to embrace this sixth sense and study it.

Now I give readings and teach mediumship development at a metaphysical shop and apothecary in North Hollywood, California; lead ghost hunts for a paranormal streaming network; and host séances.

I genuinely believe we're all born with the innate ability to communicate with spirits; you don't need to hire a psychic or medium to do so. With this book, I hope to help you identify and interpret messages from loved ones and pets on the other side and provide some comfort in knowing they're still with you.

HOW TO USE THIS BOOK

Before you contact those on the other side of the veil, allow me to explain how to use this book. It's divided into two parts, followed by a tracker.

Part 1 is designed to give you all the information you'll need to get started with spirit communication. Read through part 1 in its entirety because it provides detailed descriptions of how to properly connect with the afterlife. These chapters include essential steps that will equip you with the know-how to sense and understand spirit energy, set good intentions before contacting spirits, make a connection with loved ones and pets, and maintain that connection for as long as you want.

Part 1 will also give you instructions on meditating with the spirits around you, using tools to strengthen your spiritual connection, holding a séance, interpreting different signs, and asking for spirit messages. Then, after reading part 1 thoroughly, you can use part 2 as a reference guide to help you identify and interpret the signs you've experienced from the afterlife.

The chapters in part 2 will discuss three types of signs: paranormal experiences, nature and weather, and animals. Each chapter has several examples to help you understand what you've experienced and how to decipher the intended messages from spirits.

After reading parts 1 and 2, use the tracker pages to record the signs and messages you receive. Keeping track of your interactions will help you explore your interpretations and deepen your connections to loved ones in the afterlife.

Connecting with the Afterlife

Are you excited to begin? In part 1, you'll discover the best ways to receive spirit messages. I'll share everything I've learned on my journey to becoming a professional medium—but you don't need to be a pro to do what I do.

In the first chapter, we'll focus on what spirit energy is and how to sense it, what steps you should take before connecting, how to make contact, various ways to keep those connections open, and how other cultures view the afterlife. I'll also show you how to use various tools, such as altars and candles, to strengthen your connection and how to use meditation to better prepare yourself and sense the spirits around you.

Then, in chapter 2, I'll cover how to better open your mind to receiving messages from the beyond, what types of signs you should be looking for, common blockages that can cut your connection, and how to overcome them. I'll also go over how spirits target your physical senses to make themselves known to you, tips and tricks for holding your own séance, how to ask for messages, and how to interpret them.

Chapter 1

SENSING SPIRITS

We're surrounded by spirits all the time. And I genuinely believe that every one of us can not only sense them but also communicate with them as I do. I can't even begin to tell you how much better my life has become since I tuned in to the spirit realm. I feel so much more protected, guided, and supported—and you can, too.

Honestly, you've probably already been in contact with them most of your life. If you've ever heard a voice call your name before you fall asleep, gotten chills for seemingly no reason in an unfamiliar place, or felt a pet jump on your bed when nothing was there, you've already received spirit messages.

In this chapter, I'll explain in more detail what spirit energy is, how you can feel closer to loved ones and pets you've lost, and how you, too, can read the signs from the spirits in the afterlife. They're waiting for you to make contact.

Are you ready to shake off any limiting beliefs and dive into the spirit realm with me? Well then, grab your most comfy blanket and a big mug of hot tea, and let's go!

UNDERSTANDING SPIRIT ENERGY

Everything in the known universe is energy. Even matter isn't as solid as it first appears. Under a powerful microscope, the most static object contains vast amounts of space and moving particles of energy. Our own physical bodies are mostly energy, and not only the kind you can easily measure and examine in scientific labs. We are conscious energy made manifest.

And it's not just human beings; animals and plants have conscious energy, too. Science has amassed enormous evidence supporting both animal and plant intelligence and consciousness—some beyond what we typically consider possible. For example, animals and plants seem to communicate via telepathy. We often separate ourselves from plants and animals, but we're all part of nature and we're all conscious energy.

The only difference between living energy and spiritual energy is how that conscious energy is housed. Spirits are free-floating consciousness, and they're with us all the time, watching and guiding us. All we need to do is open our minds and senses to a different frequency to connect and communicate.

It's so easy a child could do it—and many do. Children often have imaginary friends, especially before they develop language. I'm convinced these friends are spirits, and babies are naturally open to receiving them. Most of us close off our sixth sense as we learn to talk and integrate into society, but I believe we can learn to tap back into the spiritual realm. You don't need to hire someone like me; you can connect with spiritual energy yourself.

WHAT ARE SPIRIT GUIDES?

Spirit guides are disembodied entities who guide us throughout our lives, from before birth to after death. They have different names in other cultures, such as "familiars" or "guardian angels," but their role is the same: to protect us and help us fulfill our life's purpose. They can also help us connect with other spirits, especially during a séance. We all have at least one main spirit guide, and some of us have more. To meet your guides, ask them to join you and notice any changes in how you feel. Ask for their names to strengthen the bond.

SET YOUR INTENTION WHEN CONTACTING SPIRITS

Before attempting to establish a connection with loved ones and pets on the other side, it's important to set your intentions. I prefer to start by sitting in meditation with a journal, taking notes if needed. Achieving clarity of mind should be your goal to help focus your intention.

When you're ready, ask yourself what your purpose is in contacting the deceased and what you hope to gain from the experience. Be honest. It's okay if your purpose is simply to test whether you even can make contact. Most of the séances I hosted early on were done with this intention.

If you're unsure what your real purpose is or need some guidance, I have some examples for you. Your intention could be to reconnect with lost loved ones to gain or provide closure or to ask for messages and guidance. Or perhaps you want to help them ascend or ask for their help with something in your life. Or any combination thereof!

You don't have to tell anyone else what your intention is, but it's good for you to know before starting. The more prepared you are going in, the better you'll be able to interpret spirit signs and symbols. If you don't know what you want from the experience, you may miss messages or they may be too vague to decipher.

When dealing with spirits, context is everything, and setting good intentions first is the best way to control the context.

THE AFTERLIFE IN
VARIOUS TRADITIONS

The afterlife has played a significant role throughout history across many cultures. The tombs of ancient Egypt are perhaps the most famous examples of the importance of the afterlife that have been preserved from antiquity. The concept of communicating with the dead was so commonplace for ancient Egyptians that they would ask for help with mundane tasks like baking bread. *The Egyptian Book of the Dead*, a collection of spells and other writings, was created to assist the dead as they traversed the underworld, called the Duat. Souls would be tested in the Hall of Truth and if they passed, they could freely roam among the gods in the A'aru, or Field of Reeds.

The Tibetan Book of the Dead is another book intended to be read to the dead. It contains vivid descriptions of the bardo, which is an intermediary state between death and rebirth. In some forms of Buddhism, practitioners consider the afterlife as simply a gap between lives; the difference between the living world and this liminal space is minimal—one world simply gives way to the next.

Hindus also believe in a cycle of birth, death, and reincarnation, which they call samsara. Beliefs differ on how soon after death one is reborn, but there is some time spent in transition.

Christianity and Islam teach that if you hold to a certain code of beliefs and conduct in life, you're rewarded in death with an eternal afterlife in heaven. Not all traditions within those religions believe these spirits can be contacted, but some do.

HOW TO MAKE CONTACT WITH THE AFTERLIFE

Now that you have a deeper understanding of what spirit energy is and how to set good intentions before trying to make contact, it's time to learn how to contact the departed. There are numerous ways to achieve this goal across several traditions and cultures, but we'll focus on five methods that I find work best. Some may seem similar at first glance, like meditation and prayer, but they each have subtle variations, such as mindset, intention, and location.

You may be more comfortable with one type than another, or you may want to experiment with combining two or more techniques. It's not necessary to practice all of them, but you should try at least a couple different approaches to see which ones work best for you.

Personally, I find mixing a variety of methods to be the best approach, especially since some spirits seem harder to connect with than others. The more techniques you're familiar with, the better chances you have of successful communication with the spirits from whom you hope to receive signs. Don't worry if you don't get a sign right away. Keep trying!

Meditation

The first thing I tell my students to do is meditate. If you want to connect with spirits, you need to quiet your mind enough to be able to perceive messages.

Meditation is an invitation to let spirits know you're ready to communicate. Since meditation slows your mundane thoughts, it helps you not only focus on your inner world but also feel at one with the universe and have compassion for all. This raises your vibrations. As you know, everything is energy, and energy isn't static. It's always moving, or vibrating. Mediums often use the term "vibrations" when discussing our energy fields or auras to denote this quality of being in flux.

Spirits are believed to vibrate at a higher frequency than the living, so we need to raise our vibrations to meet them. Meditation can help you achieve this.

Prayer

Prayer is similar to meditation, except for one major difference: intention. While meditation opens you up to have any kind of spirit encounter, prayer often has a specific intention. Across all traditions, the focus of prayer is most likely to ask for assistance or guidance. So if meditation is to invite, prayer is to ask.

Prayer doesn't need to be religious or ritualistic. All you need to do is focus your question to whomever you choose. Spirits love to be asked to do things for you, so don't be shy—ask away!

Dreams

Dreams are our portals to the land of the dead. When we sleep, our vibrations are naturally raised. All the outside noise quiets and the analytical mind switches gears to embrace symbolism. Spirits love to communicate through symbols, especially in our dreams; it's the easiest way for them to connect with you without you having to do much other than get a good night's sleep.

Because dreams can be so highly symbolic, I recommend keeping a dream journal and making entries about your most vivid dreams, as they're usually indicative of a spirit visitation. Make a note of anything they tell you.

MEDITATE WITH
THE SPIRITS AROUND YOU

The most common misunderstanding about meditation is that you need to sit in silence with no thoughts in your head, which results in a lot of people feeling frustrated and abandoning the practice. But anything done mindfully can be meditation, even washing the dishes. Here are some steps to help you meditate with the spirits around you. You could read them aloud while recording on your phone and then play them back so you can close your eyes and listen while meditating.

1. Sit or lie comfortably. Let your body and mind relax. Breathe deeply, paying attention to your inhalation and exhalation. Focus on making your breaths be of equal length. Breathe in for four counts, hold for four, out for four, and hold for four. Repeat four times. Gently roll your head in one direction, and then the other. Relax your neck and shoulders. Release any tension in your face and jaw muscles. Allow your vision to focus on your mind's eye.

2. Imagine pure energy rising from the ground below you, cradling you in Earth's gravity. Let all your worries and fears disappear into the dirt.

Feel this cleansing energy move up through your legs, calming your stomach, clearing away any remaining stress or obstacles. Feel this energy move through your heart, filling you with unconditional love. Then feel as it moves up and out the top of your head, allowing you to connect with your spirit guides. Picture this energy cascading down around you in a shimmering waterfall, enclosing you in a protective bubble of light. You're safe and ready to connect with spirits.

3. Say the names of those you wish to contact, whether they're loved ones or pets, and ask them to join you. Speak to them freely, telling or asking them anything you want. Wait a moment after any questions for a response. These may be visions in your mind, words you hear, or feelings in your heart or body. They may touch you or knock on a nearby surface. Keep your senses sharp and aware.

4. When you're ready, thank them for joining you, and slowly breathe yourself back into the material realm.

Spirit Scribbling

In high school, I would doodle in the margins of my notebooks. I never thought much about it until years later when I looked at those doodles again. In addition to drawings and poems, there were repeated patterns and phrases that seemed more like messages than anything else.

I still practice this today, except more mindfully. I try to shut off the language part of my brain that's preoccupied with the day's tasks and allow my hand to freely draw or write without judgment. Sometimes I'll ask specific questions and then wait to see if my hand answers. Often it does.

Being in Nature

Turn off your phone, find a comfortable spot in nature, allow your thoughts to settle, and simply be. Pay attention to your surroundings. Notice the trees. Hear the birds and insects. Smell the air. Feel the breeze.

Sometimes wind is only wind, but sometimes it's a spirit message. It can carry birdsong, feathers, butterflies, or flower petals, and sometimes it can stir up and swirl around you on an otherwise calm day. After I lost a beloved cat, Sam, every time I went to his favorite spot in the yard, the leaves would flutter, and I instinctively knew it was a sign from him.

WAYS TO STAY CONNECTED TO LOVED ONES

Once you've established a connection with a loved one or pet who has passed on, you'll want to keep that line of communication open. There are many ways to stay connected.

Because everything is energy, everything has an aura. Auras are electromagnetic energy. They have existed as a concept throughout history—from orbs in ancient Egypt and halos in Hellenistic and Roman art to chi in China and prana in India. Not only do living people have auras, but so do animals, plants, spirits, places, inanimate objects, significant dates, and sounds.

When we hold or wear something, visit a special location, listen to a favorite song, or celebrate a significant date, we mix our aura with that of the item, place, sound, or time.

Many mediums tap into their clairsentience, or clear feeling—the ability to discern auras and energy—and practice psychometry—the ability to read information from objects and other things by touching them or perceiving them—and so can you. I'll share a few examples in more detail next, but remember that this list is not exhaustive and you don't have to do any specific rituals to maintain contact with a loved one. All you need is a clear intention and an open mind.

Keep a Memento Close

My favorite keepsakes to stay connected with the deceased are objects the person or pet wore, such as jewelry or a collar. Clothes, blankets, pet beds, and toys will work well, too.

Photographs can also help create a link to a loved one because they are drawn to their likeness, since the photo captures the essence of their spirit. Also, because spirits no longer have bodies, they're attracted to objects that represent bodies, like paintings, drawings, and sculptures—even mannequins!

Simply holding the item or photo while meditating is an excellent way to practice staying connected.

Acknowledge Birthdays or Anniversaries

Spirits are drawn to significant dates. Many of my mediumship clients set up appointments that coincide with birthdays and other special dates because they already sense their loved ones but doubt themselves, so they hire me to validate their experiences. I love my job, so I don't mind that they reach out, but they don't really need me; they're already making contact.

Establish a time to celebrate the deceased. Set an extra dinner plate on their birthday, or buy some flowers for their anniversary. Allow yourself to feel their presence and send them love or gratitude in return. They will feel it.

Visit Their Places of Rest, Birth, or Somewhere They Loved

After my grandfather died, my mother visited a place by the ocean that he loved. She wondered if he knew she was there. Immediately after this thought, a seal surfaced from beneath the water. She knew it was a sign that he was there with her, and it filled her with a sense of calm.

Spirits are everywhere, but places they're connected to in life or death boost their energy. If you want to strengthen and maintain your connection, visit the places where they were born and raised, a favorite vacation spot, or where they're laid to rest. Ask for a sign and be ready to receive it.

Play Their Favorite Music or Sing and Talk to Them

Spirits are extremely attracted to sound. Many gifted mediums use their clairaudience to hear phantom voices, music, and other sounds. An excellent way to develop this ability and maintain the connection with loved ones and pets is to use sound to draw them to you and then listen for a response.

With pets, shake their treat containers or food bowls, call their names and nicknames, or jingle their leash. With loved ones, play their favorite music or sing to them, chant their names, and talk to them as if they were still living. They're always listening, and they love to hear your voice.

TOOLS FOR STRENGTHENING YOUR SPIRITUAL CONNECTION

In addition to the methods you've learned so far for making and maintaining contact with the dearly departed—from meditation and prayer to mementos and significant dates—there are tools you can use to help boost your connection to the afterlife. The following are a few examples, but this list is by no means exhaustive or even necessary. All you truly need to make contact is an open mind. However, I find that when you're first starting to connect with the other side, tools can help you focus your energy and intentions and clarify answers to important questions you may have for the deceased.

Although some tools are intended simply to attract spiritual connection, others can help you decipher signs. For example, you might sense a message but be unsure if it's your imagination playing tricks on you. Using a tool like a pendulum to ask the spirits whether it was a message can help. Other times you may feel completely disconnected; luckily, there are tools to help strengthen your spiritual connection. Here are a few of the tools you can use to clarify messages and connections.

Altars

Altars are an excellent way to maintain and boost your connection to spirits, and many cultures and religions have used some version throughout history—and still do. An altar can be where you keep your photos and other mementos of loved ones and pets as well as a focal point for your meditation.

You can also leave offerings, such as their favorite treat or drink, flowers, money, or any other trinket you find that you associate with the deceased. Depending on how much space you have, altars can be expansive or compact; they can even be kept in a travel box to be set up only when needed.

Candles

The light and energy candles emit attract spirits. Flickering or sparking flames usually indicate the presence of spirits. With little effort on their part, they can manipulate the flames to communicate with you, especially after you've established a language with them: for example, a tall flame for yes and small for no.

You can also use the flame as a focal point for meditation to stimulate your clairvoyance and practice receiving symbols. Watch the flame for twenty seconds; then close your eyes and focus on the imprint in your mind's eye. If it morphs into a recognizable shape, that could be a sign.

Crystal Balls, Mirrors, and Crystals

While crystal balls, be they glass or crystal, are a common cliché in the entertainment industry, they do attract spirits. Spirits are attracted to crossroads, and glass is a crossroad of elements. Glass contains all the elements: You need lightning (fire) striking through the sky (air) to make ocean-worn (water) sand (earth) create glass. Thus, anything made from glass will boost your connection—although spirits seem particularly drawn to crystal balls, which you can then scry, or use to look for signs and messages within the ball. Mirrors are also perfect for this purpose.

Crystals and rocks attract spirits, too. You can create a crystal grid by setting your crystals in a pattern or simply holding them in your hand while meditating. Excellent crystals for connecting with spirits are amethyst, angelite, celestite, clear quartz, Libyan desert glass, lemurian quartz, moldavite, and selenite.

Dowsing Rods and Pendulums

I love using dowsing rods and pendulums during séances and ghost hunts for obvious responses to yes or no questions. They work similarly but have different uses. Pendulums are best when communicating alone due to their subtle movements, while dowsing rods are perfect for groups. Both need to be calibrated before use.

That means you establish the movements for yes and no before asking any questions. Hold the tool in your hands, steady yourself, say, "Show me yes," and then wait for the pendulum or rods to move. Then repeat for no. Be sure to thank the spirits when you're done.

REMEMBER TO LIVE IN THE MOMENT

When you first start noticing signs from the afterlife, you may feel a little unsure and overwhelmed. It's important not to lose yourself in the experience. Their intention is not to steer you off course but rather to aid you in being the best version of yourself. They don't want you to be so consumed by grief or the desire to connect that you lose sight of what's important in the physical world.

Sometimes we want to connect with a lost loved one because we need closure or we simply miss them, but we should always remember to live in the moment. Just because spirits surround us, always protecting us, guiding us, and sending us messages, doesn't mean we should singularly focus on them and forget to live life for ourselves. Spirits want us to be happy and healthy. They want us to live our lives to the fullest and will do everything in their power to help us achieve all our heart's desires. All we need to do is ask, listen, and remember to be in the now.

Pablo Picasso said, "Every child is an artist. The problem is how to remain an artist once [they grow] up." I believe the same can be said of psychic-mediums. We're all born with this ability and can tap back into it. You don't need to hire someone like me to connect with the afterlife.

So far in chapter 1, we've covered everything you need to know to begin your journey contacting loved ones and pets on the other side. Here are the key takeaways:

- Spirits are free-floating conscious energy who are always with us—watching and guiding—and anyone can communicate with them. For the most part, spirits want to see us shine and manifest our dreams.

- Always set clear intentions when contacting spirits so you can better identify and interpret any messages received.

- Experiment with various ways to make contact, such as meditation, prayer, dreams, spirit scribbling, and being in nature, to see which methods work best for you.

- Once you've established contact, you can use a memento or photo, special dates, significant locations, or their favorite music to stay connected.

- Try different tools to strengthen your spiritual connection, such as altars, candles, crystal balls, and dowsing rods or pendulums. Be sure to ask clear yes or no questions for the latter two.

Chapter 2

INTERPRETING SIGNS FROM THE AFTERLIFE

Now that you've learned how to contact the other side, you're ready to learn how to interpret the messages you receive. Most of us spend our whole lives completely unaware we're receiving spirit signs, or we might suspect but never take it seriously. I was like that for a long time. Despite having many experiences, from seeing my deceased grandfather to getting chills on side streets in Salem, Massachusetts, I dismissed most of them as flights of fancy. However, signs are more than mere imagination.

One way to test this is to try to change some detail of the sign you receive. For example, if you ask spirits for a message and find you are picturing a purple iris, change it in your mind to white. If the color transforms easily, it's most likely your imagination. But if it keeps reverting to purple or won't let you alter it at all, it's probably a sign from the afterlife.

In this chapter, you'll learn how to keep an open mind while remaining grounded, types of signs to look for, common spiritual blockages that can cut your connection, when signs can appear, how they affect your senses, how to host your own séance, and how to ask for messages from the dead.

OPEN YOUR MIND TO MESSAGES FROM BEYOND

The most important way to approach interpreting and identifying signs from the afterlife is with an open mind. You don't have to subscribe to any specific belief system about the afterlife; simply allow for the possibility that those who've passed on retain enough conscious energy to be able to communicate with you.

However, it's perfectly okay to have some skepticism. You want to keep yourself grounded in reality and the material world, but you don't want to be so skeptical that you close yourself off from potential connections with loved ones and pets on the other side. Thus, a healthy balance of both an open mind and a dose of realism works best.

For example, say you're hosting a séance and feel a breeze. You'll want to keep an open mind to allow for the chance that it could be a spirit, so don't immediately dismiss it as nothing without further examination. Yet you also shouldn't jump to the conclusion that it's a spirit. Instead, take a moment to investigate a possible physical world source, like an open window, a fan, or an AC vent. If you don't find a logical source for the breeze, see if you can replicate the experience. If you were asking a question when you felt the wind, ask again. Or if it arose out of nowhere without a prompt, ask the spirit to do it again.

Having an open mind keeps you open to receiving so you don't miss signs you might otherwise easily dismiss.

TYPES OF SIGNS TO LOOK FOR

Spirits, being conscious energies, can affect nearly everything in both the material and astral realms. They're only restricted by the amount of energy they have access to and our ability to perceive them. All we need to do is open our senses.

We're constantly surrounded by signs from the afterlife, whether we realize we are or not, just as we're surrounded by spirits all the time. They want to connect with us and help guide us, so they'll drop clues and messages along our path. Sometimes those signs are simple synchronicities, like déjà vu or angel numbers (repeated numbers, like 11:11, or numbers in a sequence, like 12:34), which many consider messages from angels or spirits, especially if you see the same numbers several times over a period of time. But sometimes they're more tangible signs, from the mundane to the paranormal.

Signs can manifest in the physical world as animals that cross your path, sudden weather changes, or paranormal experiences such as phantom scents, electrical disturbances, or finding money or feathers.

The myriad types of signs to look for are vast and limited only by your imagination and senses. Here you'll find a brief explanation of three common categories of signs as well as some examples to help you begin to identify them when they appear. (You'll find more examples of these types of signs in part 2.) Remember to always check for ordinary, worldly sources first.

Since spirits are conscious energy and not living beings, they vibrate at a higher frequency than we do, often limiting their communication to symbols. This form of communication helps them conserve energy and makes it easier for them to connect. Thus, you should focus on interpreting any messages or signs received symbolically, not literally.

Paranormal Experiences

Paranormal experiences are anything that happens while you're asking for signs from the afterlife that you can't reasonably explain. Examples of this include but are not limited to feeling chills when there's no draft, lights flickering for no obvious reason, phantom scents without a source, and electrical devices stopping. They could also be objects moving seemingly on their own or items appearing out of the blue, like feathers or money. Feathers have long symbolized the spirit realm due to their association with angels, and throughout history there have been tales of coins falling from the sky as in the expression "pennies from heaven."

Once you've established that a sign relates to a loved one or pet, it's wise to acknowledge them every time you experience that sign to strengthen your bond with them.

COMMON SPIRITUAL BLOCKAGES
THAT CAN CUT YOUR CONNECTION

Often, clients will book me for a mediumship reading because they feel blocked, even if their minds are open to the idea of connecting to the other side and they're ready to connect. Being blocked is a perfectly normal feeling that we all experience from time to time. There are many common spiritual blockages that can either negatively affect your ability to connect or accidentally cut your connections.

The most common blockage is grief. Often, we tell ourselves we want a sign, but deep down we're still too emotional about the loss. Other common blockages include stress, negative self-talk, overthinking, trauma, doubt, headaches, insomnia, malnourishment, anger, guilt, shame, resentment, lying, jealousy, social anxiety, and fear.

The good news is that all these blockages can be cleared using a variety of techniques. Meditation is the best way, but sometimes you may not be in the right mindset to sit quietly. This is where guided meditation can work wonders for you—and there are other methods, too, like making sure you're getting enough sleep and nourishment as well as activities like yoga, spending time in nature, breathing exercises, energy healing modalities such as Reiki, practicing mindfulness, releasing negative feelings about yourself like self-doubt or other limiting beliefs, and asking your spirit guides for help.

The key thing to remember is even if you're going through a rough time and feel as if you can't connect, it's only temporary. Spirits aren't going anywhere. They'll wait until you're ready—no matter how long it takes.

Nature and Weather

Because they are energy, spirits can affect weather and nature, especially since these natural occurrences are a mix of different types of energy: thermal, kinetic, solar, and electromagnetic.

My departed cat Sam always brings a breeze when he appears. Other significant weather signs from spirits are rainbows, lightning, rain, snow, and clouds.

Another way in which spirits communicate is through nature. My grandmother's favorite flowers were violets. Shortly after she passed, my mother wondered if she was still around. That spring tons of violets blossomed all over her yard. It's never happened before or since.

Animals

The sudden appearance of animals is often a sign from the afterlife, especially if they're out of place, visit right after you ask for a message, or affect you emotionally.

Some animals are psychopomps, which is Greek for "guide of the souls." They lead spirits to the afterlife and carry messages between the living and the dead. Birds are the most common, but any creature on land, sea, or air has the potential to be a sign. The key is to notice how you were feeling when you saw the animal and if anyone from the other side popped into your head, either before or right after.

WHEN CAN SIGNS APPEAR?

Signs are around us all the time. Yet you shouldn't get so caught up in watching for signs that you don't live in the present moment or start attributing meaning to everything all the time. As you've learned, spirits want to contact us, be it to simply let us know they're there or to send specific messages or guidance. It's important to remember that the signs they send are often associated with the departed individual or pet in some way to help you understand and know exactly who is sending the message.

For example, my grandmother always told me that if she could come back as anything, she'd want to be a mockingbird because they can sing any birdsong. Shortly after I bought my house, a mockingbird appeared in our yard and stayed. She always greets me with chirps when I go outside and even mimics my whistles. I know she's a sign from my grandmother that I'm watched and protected in my home and that I'm on the right path. I didn't ask her consciously, but I probably wondered if I did the right thing in buying my house. Having that mockingbird move into my big tree confirmed that for me.

So keep your eyes and ears open no matter where you go or what you do for potential signs from the afterlife, and remember to connect them with a loved one or pet so you know who's making contact.

SIGNS CAN AFFECT YOUR SENSES

When spirits contact us, they try all our senses, hoping one will work so we can perceive their presence. This is called "clair senses," as in clairtangency, clairsentience, clairvoyance, clairaudience, clairalience, and clairgustance. There are more, but we'll focus on these for now.

The prefix "clair" is French for "clear," so each word means "clear" plus the sense. So clairvoyance means "clear seeing," clairaudience means "clear hearing," and so on. Thus, each of the clairs means to experience the sense clearly, or supernaturally, above and beyond your normal senses.

Spirits use your innate gifts to communicate with you. The more you develop your psychic abilities, the better spirits can make contact. They'll test which of your clairs is your dominant one, so it's good to know which you were born with a natural aptitude for and which you'll need to develop. A good experiment by which to learn this is to go to an unfamiliar location, take a moment to use all your senses to experience the place, and then close your eyes and ask yourself what pops into your mind first. Was it something you heard? Something you saw? Something you smelled?

Here I'll explain how spirits might target each sense to help you better develop your own abilities.

Touch

Clairtangency, or "clear touch," is when you touch an object and receive information about it. Clairsentience, or "clear feeling," is when you sense in your body the energy of a person, animal, place, or spirit.

Clairsentience can take many forms, but one of the more common is clairempathy, when you feel the emotions of another as if they were your own. Other sensations may be more physical, like how the spirit died. If these feelings become too intense, let the spirit know you understand and ask them to back off without breaking contact. Clairsentience can also present itself as chills, nausea, pain, temperature changes, or a sense of being touched.

Sight

Clairvoyance, or "clear seeing," is similar to how memory or daydreaming works. You'll see a picture in your mind's eye, like a movie. That vision could be of a person who passed, an action they took from their point of view, an object or place associated with them, or something symbolic. Other examples of clairvoyance are seeing sparks of light like dots or orbs, seeing auras, having lucid or prophetic dreams, and seeing shadow people.

Spirits love to communicate in symbols because it's easier for them and they can send complicated concepts with less energy. Over time, you can establish your own spirit vocabulary as a sort of shorthand.

Hearing

Clairaudience, or "clear hearing," is the ability to hear phantom sounds. Sometimes these sounds are inside your head; other times, they're a whisper outside your ear. It can be likened to hearing your own thoughts, but you're aware that what you're hearing isn't coming from you—the sounds feel different. You might hear buzzing sounds or high-pitched frequencies, experience a change in ear pressure or popping, or hear disembodied voices or other sounds. These sounds could be like the ones made by animals, weather, nature, machines, or music. Or clairaudience can be like tuning to a static-filled radio station where you must adjust a dial to hear better, but then sometimes it comes through crystal clear.

HOW TO HOLD A SÉANCE

I first started holding séances alone in my bedroom as a preteen using a Ouija board (also known as a talking board or spirit board), so anyone with any level of mediumship experience can as well. However, one should be mindful to follow certain measures to ensure proper protection and intention when doing so. While there are many ways to hold a séance, here's a basic step-by-step guide for hosting your own, either solo or in a group.

1. Set your intentions. Is there a person or pet you hope to communicate with? Do you have questions you want to ask?

2. Choose a location and check it for drafts or sounds first; then cleanse the space by burning lavender incense or sprinkling rosewater in a clockwise circle. Then set up a table and chairs. Add a crystal ball or grid or fresh flowers nearby, and light a candle.

3. Choose which tools to use, such as dowsing rods, spirit boxes (radios that constantly scan frequencies to assist spirits in communicating), séance trumpets (aluminum cones used to boost spirit voices), or talking boards (boards inscribed with letters and numbers that come with a pointing tool, called a

planchette, for spirits to guide in spelling out messages). You can also use the table to communicate in a Victorian practice called table-tipping, wherein the spirit either rocks the table or knocks on it to answer questions.

4. Do the meditation in chapter 1 (page 10), and be sure to envision being in a protective bubble of light. Ask your spirit guides to assist.

5. Ring a bell or make some other sound to indicate that the séance has begun. You can also say, "The veil is now lifted!"

6. If you're using tools, calibrate them now; then begin asking questions like "Are there any spirits here?" or "Please make yourself known by using any of these tools, by flickering the lights, or by rocking or knocking on the table." Ask for their name, how they died, and if they have any messages for anyone.

7. Close the session by snuffing out the candle and grounding yourself by picturing cords of light extending from your feet into the Earth. Tap the table three times and thank the spirits for communicating with you.

Smell

Clairalience, or "clear smelling," is when you smell a scent that you can't locate the source of—a phantom scent. The scent of roses or other floral fragrances are one of the most common clairalience experiences people have when spirits are active, but many also smell smoke, especially if whoever passed was a smoker. Another common scent is the dearly departed's favorite perfume or cologne. You may also smell your pet or their favorite food. Sometimes a scent is merely symbolic and not the actual thing. For example, you might smell roses because the spirit is named Rose.

Taste

Clairgustance, or "clear tasting," is when you taste something without putting it in your mouth. It's more than a simple craving because sometimes the tastes are unpleasant or something you wouldn't normally eat, like blood.

For example, you might taste what the spirit tasted at the time of their passing, or you might taste their favorite food or drink. Sometimes there's a crossover with scent and you end up tasting their favorite perfume or flowers instead of or in addition to smelling them. If the person who passed was a cook, you might even taste ingredients that you need to add while preparing food.

INTERPRETING OMENS FROM SIGNS

The words "omen" and "sign" are often used interchangeably, but there is a subtle difference. A sign is usually just a way for a spirit to make its presence known to you. This book provides extensive information on how these signs can be presented to you, how you might experience them, and how to interpret them, but a sign is simply a message or signal from spirits.

An omen, also known as a portent, is used for divination or fortune-telling. It can be a warning, a caution, or merely a heads-up about some future event or circumstance.

Also, signs tend to be specific to the spirit. They can be common signs like smelling roses but also totally unique like always hearing yodeling because your grandmother, for example, loved *The Sound of Music*. Omens, on the other hand, tend to be very specific in nature yet unrelated to the sender or receiver. Common omens throughout antiquity are eclipses; cloud formations; odd weather patterns; specific types of birds or flight patterns; the appearance of certain animals such as cats, snakes, frogs, butterflies, or rabbits; and the way in which a tree grows or if an oak drops an acorn in front of you.

Signs aren't usually negative, while omens are often viewed as bad luck; however, both are neutral. Omens don't always portend bad luck. Sometimes, they can predict something positive. So the next time a black cat crosses your path, remember that it can mean good luck, too.

ASKING FOR MESSAGES FROM THE AFTERLIFE

On a plane ride across the United States, my seatmate started chatting with me because I happened to be watching a movie that his daughter starred in. He asked me what I did for a living, and when I told him I worked as a medium, he lit up. He explained that in his culture the living interact with the dead as if they're still living, and ancestors are a very important part of the family unit. He explained that they also maintain altars and ask ancestors questions all the time. He told me these spirits are watching and waiting around for us to ask them to do something; all they want to do is help us as best they can from the other side.

I took his words to heart and have integrated them into my practice and teachings. While the spirits are happy and ready to help, they may not always know what you truly want, so it's best to state clearly how you want them to assist you.

Also, when you ask your loved ones or pets to show you a sign from the afterlife, you may not always receive one. That doesn't mean they aren't present or don't want to answer you. Often they have shown you signs, but they were subtle or unexpected, so you missed them. Or you're blocked for some reason. Regardless, don't give up. When you're ready to connect, you will, and the signs will become easier to identify and interpret with time and practice.

KEY TAKEAWAYS

The first time I ever hosted a séance, I called on a deceased friend who'd written a psychic book. After I asked her to join us, a book moved on a shelf. When I went to see which book, it was one on how to be a psychic! But signs aren't always that easy to interpret. Here are some key takeaways.

* Signs from the afterlife are around you all the time, and all you need to begin identifying them is to have an open mind and be ready to receive.

* There are many types of signs that range from paranormal experiences, odd weather patterns, and strange occurrences in nature to the appearance of

certain animals. Sometimes signs are omens, which foretell events or circumstances.

- Focus on interpreting any messages or signs you receive symbolically, not literally.

- Sometimes you're blocked from perceiving signs, but this is only temporary; there are many ways to overcome it, from meditation to a better night's sleep.

- Spirits use your senses to communicate with you in the form of clairtangency, clairsentience, clairvoyance, clairaudience, clairalience, and clairgustance. Developing these clear senses further will help you better connect.

- Your loved ones and pets are watching and waiting for you to ask them for messages and guidance. All you need to do is be open, clear, and direct.

PART TWO

Signs from the Afterlife

In part 2, I hope to give you the answers you seek in interpreting signs from your loved ones, both humans and pets.

We're going to look at paranormal experiences, nature and weather, and animals. I'll give you fifteen of the more common examples of each sign. Use each example as a launchpad to assist you in finding your own interpretation.

Please bear in mind that signs can be difficult to define. Often a sign can mean vastly different things to different people. I'll try to offer as many variations as possible, but you should also take the time to dig deeper and find your own unique meaning for every sign you encounter.

Spirits prefer to communicate using symbolism. Remember that spirit signs are often only symbolic and are not meant to be taken as literal messages from the afterlife.

Chapter 3

PARANORMAL
EXPERIENCES

The first time I officially investigated a location for paranormal activity was at the Los Angeles Police Museum for a live streaming event on The Dark Zone Network. I was so nervous! There were several cameras and lights pointed at me. As soon as they went live, I had a moment of panic: *What if my gifts suddenly stop working?* Then I reminded myself that the ability to communicate with the dead is not about me. Anyone can do this. I turned off my ego mind and allowed myself to follow my instincts, and, wow, we got a lot of paranormal experiences!

In this section, I'll share fifteen examples of para-normal events you might encounter and what they could mean. I'll include variations on how you can interpret these messages and the many ways each sign may present itself. For example, electrical disturbances could be your lights flickering or your TV channels changing independently.

Remember, none of these interpretations are exhaustive. Use your intuition to discern which feels the most correct for you. Simply read the sign and ask aloud, "Does this feel true?" Then wait for a response of yes or no from your spirit guides or the spirit from which you received the sign.

AURAS ⁖

Auras are visual representations of our electromagnetic energy—our astral selves. If you see colors or sparks of light coming off people, animals, plants, or objects, you're seeing their auras. Auras are believed to hold information about our past (including past lives), present, and future. But auras aren't only for the material world; spirits have auras, too. Sometimes when we see, either in our mind's eye or in the physical world, flashes of light or translucent shapes like orbs, we're seeing the aura of a spirit. Often, seeing a spirit's aura means you're dealing with sentient energy and not merely an energetic echo (non-sentient spiritual energy left over from a previous traumatic or impactful event).

Edgar Cayce, one of the most prolific American psychics of the twentieth century, concluded through his foundation, Association for Research and Enlightenment (ARE), that the colors or shapes you see in an aura reveal things about the spirit associated with it. Bright, jagged lines shooting out like fireworks could indicate a creative or great thinker. Dark, heavy lines could indicate that the spirit is angry or upset. You might also perceive a dark heaviness in a particular part of their body, which could indicate how they died. Swirling lines could suggest confusion, and they might have had dementia before death.

Aura color meanings are not one-size-fits-all, though. There are a lot of charts and graphs out there that will tell you what each color means, but these are not conclusive. Different colors can mean different things to different people at different times, so it's essential to look at the whole picture when determining what a spirit's aura color means. However, here are some common examples:

- Red is anger, ego, or vitality.

- Orange is virtue or thoughtfulness.

- Yellow or gold is happiness and health.

- Green is healing and nurturing but could be jealousy.

- Blue is spiritual and creative but also moody.

- Purple is intuition.

- White is balance and harmony.

- Black, brown, or gray is depression or disease.

- Pink is love.

DREAMS ⚬

Dreams are the easiest way for spirits to send us signs. These signs could be anything, so it's important to focus on what kind of dream you had. They could be vivid dreams, meaning they're lush in color and intense in feeling. They could be lucid dreams, where you're conscious that you're dreaming, and could also coincide with astral travel dreams, where your consciousness travels outside your body to another time or place. In these dreams, you may also link up with others, either living or dead.

You could have prophetic dreams, in which you dream about a future event that eventually happens, be it personal or global. Or you could experience sleep paralysis, a hypnagogic state where you're conscious (although some believe you're dreaming) but your body is still asleep, so you can't move, and you may see apparitions.

When I was around five, I dreamed I was drinking out of a clear mug and there was a giant bug in it. Later, I found a cockroach in my ice cube at a restaurant with my family. Prophetic dreams are warnings from spirits to pay attention.

Years later, I dreamed of a friend who had passed away. In my dream, we were at an amusement park talking when suddenly everything turned shimmery, and he said, "Oh, I forgot you're still alive." These types of dreams are usually the dead wanting to reconnect.

In one sleep paralysis occurrence, I saw a shadow figure climb on top of me, holding me down. I tried to break free but couldn't. Then I heard the voice of a departed friend tell me that I had the power to fight. I asked for her help, but she said I had to do it myself. These experiences caution that while you may not feel in control, you are—step into your power!

Prophetic dreams are often accompanied by déjà vu. A spirit shows you a glimpse of your future in your dreams to either prepare you for what's to come or remind you that you're exactly where you should be. The experience of déjà vu is actually remembering the dream and acknowledging that message.

ELECTRICAL DISTURBANCES ⚡

Spirits are sentient energy, so it makes sense that they can cause all sorts of electrical disturbances such as lights flickering; appliances and other electronics turning on or off, sparking, or even exploding; cars losing power; and cameras or cell phones glitching. Spirits also show up as orbs that appear in photographs, blackouts or power surges, strange voices coming through static-filled radio stations, TV channels changing on their own, phantom text messages or static-filled phone calls, and watches or clocks stopping. Electronic devices that are not plugged in, have dead batteries, or are broken may suddenly start working, or motion detectors or security cameras may be set off even though nothing appears to be moving.

Lights flickering and other electrical disturbances could mean several things, depending on what you were feeling or what questions you were asking spirits at the time. For example, flickering lights could mean they're trying to warn you not to dwell in a dark place for too long or that they're a light in the darkness ready to guide you. Or such disturbances could mean that they're present and want to comfort or protect you. They can also be a way to get your attention to answer questions or ask for help with something they didn't finish.

You can establish a pattern to these disturbances to create binary responses, such as yes and no. This technique works well when using an electromagnetic field (EMF) detector in paranormal investigations. The device lights up when it detects electromagnetic fields, which spirits are believed to generate and manipulate. One way to determine if that energy is sentient would be to ask the deceased to make the lights on the device go on for yes and stay off for no and then repeat questions to test whether you get the same results every time.

Remember, always rule out the mundane first and get your wiring checked before assuming it's spirits!

EMOTIONAL REACTIONS ⋄

Clairempathy is when you feel an emotion that is not your own. It could be from a spirit, person, animal, plant, object, or even place. It's an offshoot of clairsentience, but I like to separate it because clairsentience can be very broad in how you sense things, whereas clairempathy is very specifically feeling emotions. Most everyone feels empathy; for example, we feel compassion for someone when we witness them going through turmoil or pain. Clairempathy, though, is when we take on the emotions of others without any obvious sign or visual clue about what they feel, as if their feelings were our own. Sometimes you may be confused about why you're feeling what you're feeling—that's clairempathy.

During one of the paranormal investigations of the Los Angeles Police Museum, I suddenly felt overwhelming sadness so strongly that I had to stop and sit down. I also felt as if I was pregnant and in intense pain, like being stabbed in my belly. (This is clairsentience.) Once the physical sensations passed, the emotions remained and grew stronger. I was fighting back the tears. The team believed I was channeling a celebrity who died traumatically and whose items tied to the incident are stored in the museum.

When spirits do this, they want to connect with us on an emotional level. They want us to know either how they felt when they died or how they feel now in the afterlife.

If the emotions are too strong or unpleasant, imagine yourself in a protective bubble and ask the spirit to ease off.

You may also feel an intense amount of love in your heart, which is often spirits showing you how much you're loved and supported from the other side.

FEELING TOUCH ⁓

Feeling as if you are touched when no one is there is a widespread paranormal phenomenon. It could happen while you are lying down, sitting, walking, or doing just about anything. You may feel someone gently pat the top of your head, stroke your arm or back, rest their hand on your shoulder, or brush past you. They might pull or stroke your hair or clothes or even push you, which happened to me once at a haunted mausoleum in California after a fellow paranormal investigator used flash photography directly after I heard the spirits request that we not use it. (We ran out of there so fast!) If they pull your hair or clothes, they're trying to get your attention, but if they push you, they're trying to warn you of their boundaries.

In the introduction, I mentioned an encounter with a departed friend in which I felt her hand touch my shoulder. Before she did so, I was on the verge of hyperventilating. I was so upset but the moment she touched me, a sense of calm washed over me and I caught my breath. Her spirit touch was comforting beyond anything in the material world.

You might also feel something climb onto your bed, paw at your feet, knead you, or curl up next to you, which are all signs from beloved pets who've crossed over.

In almost all cases of being touched by spirits, be they humans or pets, they're sending you a message of comfort. They want to console you when you're grieving them, soothe you when you're dealing with difficulties, and bolster your heart to face another day. They also want to remind you that they're still with you—you are not alone and are loved unconditionally.

NUMBERS

Seeing numbers can be a sign from the afterlife. These can be repeating or sequential numbers, also known as angel numbers, like 222, 333, or 11:11 or 12:34 on a clock. Or the numbers could be significant dates like birthdays or anniversaries. You can experience paranormal events at the same time every day or night. (The most active times for spirits are between midnight and 4 a.m., known as the witching hour, a designated time in folklore when supernatural events occur.)

Numerous books list extensive meanings for each angel number. However, in my experience, any time you see these repeated or sequential numbers, they represent synchronicity, which Carl Jung, an early-twentieth-century Swiss psychiatrist, described as coincidental events that seem related but aren't. I take it a step further and insist they are related. Repeated or sequential numbers are a sign from the spirits that you are on the right path. They assure you that you should keep going, even if times are hard or not exactly how you'd prefer them to be.

If you're experiencing a paranormal event at the same time every night, take note of the time and try to connect with spirits the next time it occurs. They're trying to communicate with you, so ask them if they can send you a clearer message.

If the numbers correlate to particular dates, you most likely know exactly who's reaching out, whether they're human or animal. They want to say hello and let you know they're visiting. You could acknowledge the occasion with an offering or say hello back.

There's also a belief that these synchronicities with repeating numbers are an excellent time to make a wish, so tell the spirits what your heart desires most!

OBJECTS APPEARING ⁂

Sometimes objects appear out of the blue, or apparate. When something apparates, it teleports by dematerializing in one location and rematerializing elsewhere. These items, or apports, can be from your past, something you've never seen before, or something that appeared on your path but you didn't pick up at the time.

These could be many different types of objects, from the more common feathers and money to all kinds of things like rocks, shells, jewelry, flowers, talismans, religious figurines, books, photos, playing cards, or other trinkets. They could also be live animals or divination tools like talking boards, tarot cards, or pendulums.

One of the oldest tricks in the book of fake mediums in the 1800s, especially during the heyday of Spiritualism (a religion centered on contacting the dead), was making things apparate. While many of these events were found to be scams, the phenomenon of objects appearing is genuine. Often the items have personal significance to the spirit, you, or both. For example, when I was going through a rough time and asked for a sign from my grandmother, I found an arrowhead in my house that I'd never seen before. She and I used to find arrowheads all the time in her backyard when I was little.

If the object that appears is from your past, the spirit is telling you that it's okay to move on. If you were taking a walk and a feather appeared in your path, you didn't pick it up, and then you found it later in a pocket, it was a gift to let you know you're protected, guided, and supported by the afterlife. If you find divination tools, they want to send you a message and hope these items will help. Money usually represents prosperity, abundance, or good fortune coming your way. Rocks could mean you need grounding. Talismans and religious figurines suggest you're protected. Books offer guidance.

OBJECTS MOVING ⁖

Objects might move, float, or balance oddly; be missing; or be found in strange places. I'm referring here to objects you already own. For example, my stepmom lost her wedding ring from her first marriage decades prior. Later, my dad, her second husband, found it in an unlikely place in a different house and state than where it was lost after receiving a clairvoyant message of it being in a pill bottle.

These objects could be anything from something large like furniture or wall decorations to small items like belt buckles, jewelry, remote controls, crystals, and other trinkets or shiny objects. Books or keepsakes might fly from shelves, and framed photos might fall off the wall. Walls and shelves might shake when there's no earthquake. Doors or cabinets might open, close, lock, or unlock independently. Swings or rocking chairs might move when there's no wind or fan. Depressions could appear on beds, couches, or carpets.

When an object moves in any of these ways, the spirit is trying to draw your attention to the item for a specific reason. When opening or unlocking doors, it could be to tell you to try to open your eyes or mind or try something new. When closing or locking, it could be trying to warn you that something isn't right for you.

When items go missing, they usually end up somewhere else, and I often chalk this up to the fact that the spirit wanted something of yours for a while, most likely to better bond with you. If depressions appear on soft surfaces, especially after you've dreamed of someone who passed, they're that spirit visiting you, especially pets on beds. If you're about to sleep or wake up, they know you'll be easier to communicate with, so they choose these times to visit and are most likely offering you comfort.

With books, pay attention to the title and topic. When my deceased friend moved a book on how to be a psychic, I knew it was a sign from her (she had written a similar book) and also that she was telling me to start taking mediumship seriously and study how to be a better one.

PHANTOM FLAVORS ⁝

One of the weirdest paranormal experiences I've encountered in all my years of practice has been clairgustance, or intuitive taste, which is when you taste something that isn't in your mouth or in your physical presence at all. It's also considered one of the rarest clear senses, though I can't help but wonder if that's only because most people dismiss it when it happens. How often have you been going about your day when suddenly you get an odd flavor in your mouth? Perhaps you unexpectedly taste your grandma's homemade chocolate chip cookies or some old-fashioned candy you haven't seen for sale in years.

Suppose you recognize the taste and can associate it with a specific person who has passed away. In that case, it's most likely a sign from them alerting you to their presence, perhaps even reminding you of some special memory they share with you. If the person who passed was a cook, you might be tasting their specialty or even suggestions for your next meal! As with clairalience (sensing smell), it could also be a request for an offering, especially if you're tasting their favorite food or drink.

Sometimes, you may taste something unpleasant or distinctly not edible, like blood, chemicals, or sweat. In that case, you are experiencing something similar to what "medical intuitives" (a type of medium whose specialty is sensing physical ailments in others; this method should be used in addition to regular medical treatment, not in lieu of it) and other types of mediums undergo when they tap into how someone passed away and take on all of those sense experiences. The event of death is highly significant to spirits, and that's why they want to share it with you. It's not meant to be morbid or scary, but it can be overwhelming to the living. When this happens, acknowledge that you've received the message from the spirit; then tell them you no longer need to taste whatever the phantom flavor is.

PHANTOM FRAGRANCES ⚜

A scent can take you back to any point in time and help you recall it vividly, activating all your other senses. When you smell a scent you can't locate the source of, you're experiencing clairalience. A fragrance can remind you of a person or pet long gone and awaken a more profound feeling of that spirit present.

Artist and activist David Wojnarowicz wrote, "Smell the flowers while you can." The same message applies when you smell roses or other floral scents during spirit activity. They're reminding you to be in the moment and appreciate life while you're still among the living. Other fragrances like lavender can calm, cleanse, or invite spirits.

In Catholicism, there's the "odor of sanctity," which is said to be floral in nature and represents the presence of saints. Since the scent of flowers is often pleasant, it could signify joy or happiness, especially if you asked the spirit if they're okay. Or it could be an omen of love, luck, or marriage on the horizon.

Perfume, cologne, and smoke are other common phantom scents. Typically, they're tied to specific people and represent their favorite scents to wear or cigarette or pipe tobacco they used to smoke. Smelling these scents usually means that they're visiting. You may also smell food or drink. These could be a deceased's favorite cookies baking or their signature cocktail. Again, these are signs that they're stopping by to say hello and offer comfort. They might even want you to leave out a meal for them or offerings on an altar. (Tobacco makes for an excellent offering.)

You might smell wet dog, tuna, hay, or some other scent related to your beloved animals, which would indicate a visit from them to let you know they're still around you.

PHANTOM SOUNDS ✷

When you hear phantom sounds and experience clairaudience, you're perceiving noises from the spirit world. These could be in your head, as in hearing thoughts that you know are not coming from you, or they could come from outside your head and sound like a whisper or static. Or they could be electronic voice phenomena (EVPs), audible only with an audio recorder. Depending on what you hear, there can be a wide range of possible interpretations, but in essence, any phantom sound is a spirit that wants you to hear them; ask them what messages they have for you and listen.

In the mid-1800s, the Fox sisters (three early Spiritualists) claimed to hear knocks on walls and furniture that seemed to be sentient replies to questions. Years later, one of the sisters confessed to making it all up, though some doubt her claims. Regardless, knocking is a common clairaudient occurrence. Other sounds you may hear are giggling, feet running, music boxes playing, or a ball bouncing. These sounds are usually associated with deceased children who miss you or enjoy your energy and want you to play with them. You might also hear grunting, rustling, barking, meowing, or claws on hard floors, which usually indicates your beloved pets visiting to say hello and provide comfort.

Disembodied voices murmuring, calling your name—especially before you fall asleep or when you wake up—whistling, singing, coughing, and sneezing are all clear signs that someone from the afterlife wants to talk to you. You can use a spirit box (a device that helps spirits communicate through radio frequencies) to help them or an audio recorder (which records EVPs). After recording the sound, play it back to hear what the spirit is saying. You may also hear music, machinery, footsteps, nature sounds, ringing bells, or buzzing in your ears—all intended to get your attention.

PSYCHIC INSIGHT

Psychic insight is claircognizance, meaning "clear knowing," or extrasensory perception (ESP), and it happens when you know something without any explanation or reason. A flash of insight pops into your head like magic. It could be paired with any other clear sense. For example, you may have a psychic vision and know it's true.

This differs from clairsentience because you don't feel it in your body, like a gut instinct, but rather you know it in your mind. Another key difference is in the details. Often with clairsentience you might dread or anticipate a future event but not know why. With claircognizance, you understand why.

Claircognizance can be of the future (precognition), present, or past (retro-cognition). Meditation is one of the best ways to receive this type of sign, but it can also strike you when you least expect it.

There's no limit to what kind of information spirits can beam into your mind. The most common is intuition, like knowing you should take the stairs because something's wrong with the elevator. A more evident one is an artistic inspiration, when you've been stuck on a project and then suddenly know exactly what you need to do to make it work. Spirit guides often use claircognizance to guide you, and so do animals.

Animals don't often think the way we do. Many humans think in terms of language. However, all creatures can experience claircognizance. Thus, when deceased pets want you to know something, they may send it straight to your mind. In most cases, you'll know exactly what the sign is based on the information they send. But if you're unsure, they still just want you to know that they're with you.

PSYCHIC VISIONS ✂

Psychic visions or flashes, also known as clairvoyance, can happen in many ways, but essentially, you see a picture in your mind or overlaying the reality of the world outside your mind. You might see people, animals, spirits, plants, places, objects, actions, colors, shapes, symbols, or sparks of light. These visions can be of the past, present, or future. They may occur when you touch something, which would be clairtangency working in conjunction with clairvoyance.

Visions differ from dreams because you're awake, and they differ from seeing apparitions because you don't get the sense that there's a sentient being in your presence. They're more like memories being beamed into your head or your field of vision. Basically, spirits want to show you something that is important to them or you.

If you see a flash of a specific person or animal, they could be trying to contact you. Or if it occurs while touching an object, you could be seeing an echo of the person or animal who owned the item.

If you see a place, it could be connected to the spirit, such as their birthplace. It could also indicate a significant event that either took place or will take place at that location.

If you see an action, it could be something the person did for a living or something a person or animal loved to do, like cooking or playing catch, and they're reminding you or validating that it's really them.

Or you may see a shape or symbol, since that's the easiest way for spirits to send images. These could be logos, talismans, or any number of things, depending on the sender and receiver. Common shapes are hearts for love; circles for wedding rings or completion; squares for homes, rooms, boxes, or balance; triangles for tombs, ascendance, or opposites attracting; and flowers for names, events, or offerings.

SEEING APPARITIONS ⁑

While clairvoyance is often seeing a sign in your mind's eye, sometimes you might see an apparition in the material plane. These may be humanoid or symbolic.

Shadows and shadow people or silhouettes are among the more common visions, though you might even see an actual ghost. You might see specters dressed in period clothes, often repeatedly acting out battles or duels or simply pacing in front of a window. Sometimes spirits are more modern and those who witness them think they're living humans until they vanish or move through solid objects.

These visions could be tied to events and might be merely echoes—non-sentient spiritual energy—or they could be sentient entities. If they acknowledge you or respond to questions, they're sentient, but if they carry on as if you aren't even there, it's more likely just an energetic imprint of some past traumatic event. Sometimes these non-sentient energies are spirits trapped between worlds, reliving events from their lives or their deaths, and they haven't fully realized they've died or ascended to become sentient spirits. Other times they are residual energies left over from an emotional event to serve as a warning to others to avoid the same fate.

Children often see imaginary friends, but I believe these are spirits. They're usually harmless. Frequently, they're ancestors watching over their legacy—but not always. In my last apartment, I often saw a child with dark hair and red shorts appear in my bathroom, walk down the hallway, and sit in front of the TV. I later learned that a young boy had drowned in the hot tub right outside my bathroom wall.

Sometimes you may only see eyes, be they reptilian, catlike, or human. In that case, they're telling you to open your eyes and see clearly what's right in front of you because you're missing something. Or you might see sacred geometry (symbolic geometric shapes), neon grids, or other floating lines. I used to see these all the time as a kid and feel as if I was seeing the language of the universe. The message is to look beneath the surface and find the hidden meaning or source.

SENSING PRESENCES

Sensing a presence is clairsentience, or perceiving spirits by feeling them in your body. You may not see an apparition or hear anything, but you can sense that something is there. You might experience goose bumps, chills, pain, tickling, your hair standing on end, dizziness, nausea, headaches, congestion or choking, feeling as if you're rocking in a boat, a fight-or-flight response, or even icy dread, especially if you also feel like you're being watched by something outside a window or from inside a closet.

Unlike feeling touched directly by spirits, you simply sense their presence. They tend to feel more neutral in their intentions than those who would touch you for comfort or warning.

Clairsentience is one of the most common clear senses and you may have already experienced it—from having a hunch to feeling a bad vibe. These "feelings" are one of the first ways spirits try to communicate with us.

Often when we sense presences, we're only sensing the leftover trauma of some past event and not a living spirit at all, but other times they may be sentient. One way to test whether they're conscious energy is to ask them to repeat whatever you sensed. For example, if you felt chills, then ask the spirit either to make them stop or to make you feel them again. Or tell them that you acknowledge them and give them permission to send you a message in other ways, such as knocking on walls or flickering the lights. If they respond, they're spirits, but if they don't and the feeling continues regardless of your actions, it may be only an energetic echo.

When you sense them but can't seem to hear them, see them, or feel them touch you, they may be having trouble making a connection. So if they're sentient, the spirit's goal in having you sense them is to let you know that they're there and wish to make contact, which is when tools or meditation can help.

Chapter 4

NATURE AND WEATHER

Before I started writing this chapter, I stepped outside for inspiration and a breeze appeared, shaking my orange tree. I asked if it was a sign from my cat Sam, and the wind swirled around me to the olive tree behind me and then on to the avocado trees on either side. I was in the middle of a dance party with all the trees swaying around me. This is just one of the everyday little signs from spirits telling you to keep going—you're supported.

However, as with most signs, it's important to remember that interpretations vary wildly, depending on a variety of factors. I'll endeavor to give you as many variations as I have come across in research and practice, but keep in mind one key factor when interpreting nature and weather signs: What were you thinking about or asking the spirit before the sign appeared? Without this in mind, you may not be able to distinguish between a common occurrence and one that has meaning. You may have purposefully asked a spirit for a sign, or you may have wondered if you were doing the right thing. If one of the following phenomena occurred directly afterward, it's likely a sign from the afterlife.

CLOUDS ✦

Children often play games to see how many different shapes they can spot in the clouds. But these aren't merely the whimsical imaginings of youth. Clouds are signs from the afterlife, too.

The tricky thing with clouds is the limitless range of possible meanings. One could devote an entire book just to reading the skies; however, there are a few simple tricks to help narrow down the potential meanings. First, keep in mind what you asked. Second, while the shape of the cloud can hold a meaning, don't look only at the shape to decide if you're seeing a rabbit or an alien, but also consider the type of cloud—from light and fluffy to dark and ominous—as well as any other weather happening simultaneously. (For animal shapes, use chapter 5, which is about animals, to help guide you.)

Water represents emotion in many traditions, and since clouds are made of water vapor, they are emotionally linked signs as well. The nature of clouds is to obscure things, so a cloud sign represents hidden emotions. A darker cloud symbolizes deeper emotions, whereas a lighter one is more surface. Remember, too, that "every cloud has a silver lining," so whether dark or light, clouds mean there's hope.

If clouds are flat and smooth (stratus clouds), things should go smoothly. If they look like bumpy cotton balls (cumulus), there could be a bumpy road, delays, or something unexpected ahead. Wispy, thin clouds (cirrus) could mean you're missing a key element or there's not enough information. Fast-moving clouds mean change or a quick resolution is coming. Slow or still clouds could be stability or stagnation. And fog indicates confusion, lack of clarity, or blockage. If this is the case, ask spirits for help in removing any obstacles.

FEATHERS

Feathers are a very common sign from the afterlife. They represent birds, which are psychopomps—guides and messengers of the dead—as well as angels. Finding one is often considered a gift from spirits. Typically, feathers appear directly in your path—in front of your door or on your routine walk. They symbolize that you're on the right track, doing exactly what you should be doing, especially if you asked for that kind of sign or simply wondered.

After I was offered the opportunity to write this book, I wondered if it was the right thing to do. I knew I wanted to write it, but I was also teaching a mediumship series, juggling many clients, and about to travel abroad. How could I possibly squeeze in writing a book? I stepped outside for some fresh air, and on my welcome mat was a white feather. I instantly knew it was a sign that I had to do it.

While all feathers have a similar meaning, the color of the feather can offer more insight. White is typically a sign of support. Pink is for love, be it self-love, familial, platonic, or romantic. Yellow represents success. Blue is a sign that your connection to the spirit realm is strengthening. Gray brings harmony, black is protection, and a mix of colors represents transition.

Feathers also seem to be a common gift from pets; they're telling you they're okay and they're still with you.

Another interpretation of feathers is the spirit telling you to make things lighter, be gentle with yourself, and slow down. Are you resisting something and struggling as a result? Like a feather gliding on the currents of the wind, let go and go with the flow.

FLOWERS ✦

Flowers can present themselves as signs in a variety of ways. Just like when the violets bloomed after my grandmother's passing, they could be your loved one's favorite flower suddenly growing somewhere it never grew before. Or you could find a random blossom or petal on your path.

The ancient Greeks practiced floromancy, a form of divination that uses flowers to predict the future, and it's still used today. It's a complicated technique involving shape, color, stalk, aroma, and petals, among other characteristics, but aspects of floromancy can be useful in determining the meaning of a flower sign.

If the flower you find is red or pink, it can symbolize love; blue or purple can represent psychic ability, spirituality, and harmony; orange or yellow is happiness and accomplishment; green is healing and nurturing; white is protection, trust, and hope; and black indicates something hidden or powerful.

If the flower has thorns, there's a price to be paid for what you seek, but it's worth it. If there are petals missing or damaged, you're close but you still have some work to do. Flowers with a strong aroma are telling you to take the time to stop and smell them.

Specific flowers also have their own meanings. There are too many to mention them all, but I'll share a few examples of the more common ones. Irises symbolize the spiritual realm. Lilies are new beginnings. Roses are love, with red roses being romantic, pink ones friendship, yellow an apology or forgiveness, and white protection. Dandelions are transformation or wishes coming true. Daises are innocence, which could likely represent children or pets. Jasmine is knowledge and wisdom. And violets offer psychic healing and protection.

All flowers represent something inside you blossoming or a message from spirits to remember to look for beauty and goodness in the world.

MIRAGES ⁙

A mirage is a heat shimmer or haze caused by cool air meeting the hot ground. This combination creates an optical illusion that can look like an oasis in the desert or water on a highway, even when both are dry. It's a bending of the light called refraction and is similar to but different from a reflection. Mirages are naturally occurring phenomena, but they can also be caused by things like car or industrial fumes or exhaust—as well as supernatural causes. If you've asked for a sign and see a mirage directly after, a spirit is most likely sending you a message.

Since mirages are first and foremost illusions, the spirit could be telling you that you aren't seeing things as they are. This means that something you think is real or true isn't or that you're unintentionally or intentionally preventing yourself from seeing the truth. While daydreaming can be fun, if we do it too much, we lose sight of what's right in front of us, so mirages tell us to open our eyes and be present in the moment. If you don't like what you see, you have the power to change it. Don't be daunted by the big picture; instead, focus on the small details you can start changing today.

Mirages might indicate that someone you thought you knew or trusted is lying to you or presenting a false image. But they also suggest you should take time before confronting someone to cool down any anger you carry and see if your perception changes.

Mirages can mislead you, so when a spirit warns you with one, it may be time to reexamine your path or intentions. Because mirages are false images, they may be telling you to be careful how you present yourself. Remember to be your authentic self.

ICE AND SNOW

Icicles may hang from your roof as you step outside to start your day, or you might slip on the ice walking down a pathway. A nearby pond could be frozen over—you might skate on it or the ice might break. The sky could be crystal clear except for one lone snowflake that lands on you, or you might be in the middle of a blizzard. These are all common occurrences in colder climates. But if you recently asked for a sign from a loved one, they're sending you a message with ice or snow.

Since, like clouds, they're water-based, all ice and snow messages are in the province of emotions. However, since they're frozen water, they mean that it's time to thaw your heart or that you aren't in touch with your emotions. If the ice is melting, it may be time to let go of whatever's holding you back. If it breaks, introduce yourself to that certain someone—or tread lightly.

Icicles require the right conditions to form—warm enough for water to drip but cold enough to freeze—so if you spot them, they could be a sign that the timing is perfect. If they have ripples, make sure you aren't forgetting any details.

Snow and ice can also represent childhood, especially if you have fond memories of sledding or ice-skating with someone who has passed. They're showing you they remember and are with you. Spotting a single snowflake is a sign that a spirit is present and you're special to them. A snowstorm signifies that it's time to hunker down and wait it out, or it could also mean freedom in the form of a snow day. If the world is blanketed in snow, it's time to start over. The spirits have your back.

MUSHROOMS ⚘

Mushrooms are magic, and not just the ones called "magic mushrooms." They can be medicine, nourishment, or poison. What we see on the surface is only a fraction of their growth. Underground, their mycelium stretches far, interconnecting with all plant matter. They grow on trees or decaying organic matter but can pop up in your front yard. Mushrooms often appear after a rainstorm or in wet conditions, but that doesn't mean they can't be a sign, especially if they appear when there's no water around.

Sometimes they grow in circles called fairy rings, which were once believed to have appeared after the fairies danced. When I was little, my grandmother used to say that the fairies grew mushrooms so they could dance under them in the rain.

Since mushrooms both support and convert life, when they appear as a sign, they indicate that you're supported from the spirit realm while you go through a transition. They could also tell you to be cautious and use your discernment to know whether your relationship or what you're about to embark on is safe or perhaps not, especially if the mushroom you see is poisonous. However, they can also indicate a rising of consciousness or oneness with everything.

If they grow in a ring, you're surrounded by spirits. Embrace them! If they grow from a dead tree, you may experience a rebirth, or if from a living tree, it's time to step it up, especially if they look like little stairs. If they pop up in the grass, it's time to reconnect with Mother Nature.

When you see a mushroom sign, regardless of the specifics, know that you're deeply connected with spirit and Earth, and you either need to be or already are well balanced.

RAIN ⚬

Rain can be a nuisance on a day you planned to be out-doors or a relief after a drought. It can be dangerous and cause a flood, and it can be cold and hard in the form of hail or sleet. Since all forms of rain are common, rain is likely a sign from a spirit only if you asked for one and experienced the rain directly after. For example, you ask for a sign and feel a slight drizzle or hear a loud clap of thunder and see lightning strike across the sky.

If you ask for a sign and then it rains, there's a lot of emotion in your answer. (Remember, water represents emotion.) There are also several idioms about the rain that should be taken into consideration when inter-preting a sign. You could be "saving for a rainy day," complaining that "when it rains it pours," or assuring someone that you'll be there "come rain or shine." If you've been waiting for the right time to do something, rain is telling you that now is the time. If you feel like you've been experiencing a lot of misfortune, rain, through spirits, could be letting you know that things will soon change for the better, especially if the sun breaks through and clears the sky.

How it's raining can have different meanings, too. A gentle rain could mean minor frustrations and delays, but things will still work out. Driving rain could mean a lot of work will be required to get what you want or resistance will need to be overcome. Lightning could suggest a spark of inspiration, and thunder could be a reminder to listen to your heart. A hurricane warns you to slow down and take shelter for a while but also that you have access to a lot of power in the spirit realm. Hail or sleet warns you to beware of those who may appear friendly but are cold and calculating underneath.

RAINBOWS

Rainbows are my favorite signs from spirits. When I was much younger, every time I was going through some sort of turmoil, I asked whoever was listening on the other side for a sign that everything would be okay. Often, a rainbow would appear. I took that as a good sign.

Later, when I studied theology in college, I learned that rainbows are a sign that appears in the Bible. My mind was blown. While I'm sure my interest in and connection to rainbows stemmed from Kermit the Frog, here was ancient proof that rainbows are a sign from beyond.

If you ask for a message from the spirits and you see a rainbow, consider it a very good sign. If you asked about getting a job or falling in love or anything else your heart desires, the answer is an enthusiastic yes. Rainbows also offer comfort—a reminder that there is beauty in the world even amid chaos. You can't get a rainbow without rain, but you also need sunshine. Know the storm clouds will part.

Folklore tells us that leprechauns hide pots of gold at the ends of rainbows, so they can also represent prosperity, good fortune, and luck. If you see a double rainbow, know that there is hope. Don't give up.

If you ask for a sign from a pet or person and you see a rainbow, you know your loved one crossed over and is happy on the other side. Rainbows are the colorful bridge that connects the spirit realm to the earthly plane; know that your loved one will always be with you and waiting on the other side to greet you.

ROCKS ❖

Rocks come in all shapes, sizes, colors, and textures. They can be broken or smoothed by rushing water. They can be common rocks or sparkling crystals and gemstones. Spirits seem to love leaving rocks, especially departed pets. I used to care for a feral neighborhood cat named Sam who, sadly, passed before I could rescue him. I asked for signs afterward, and when I went back to his favorite spot, I found a red rock—my yard has mostly gray and white rocks—in my raised bed that no rocks could possibly "fall up" into. I knew it was a sign from Sam!

Rocks offer stability, concrete proof, and trustworthiness, as in the "salt of the earth." Rocks represent the

Earth and ground, so when you find one, it can mean a spirit is telling you that you need grounding. Maybe your head is in the clouds or you're out of touch and need to spend some time in nature to reconnect with the Earth beneath your feet.

According to my grandmother, rocks with a stripe through them will bring you good luck. If the rock is heart-shaped, the spirit wants you to know you're loved. If it's flat or smooth, you may be worrying too much, so the spirit offers you comfort with a worry stone. If it's jagged or sharp, the rock and spirit can offer you protection. If you find an arrowhead, it's a reminder to stand up and fight for yourself; embrace your inner power.

Depending on the rock's color, it could mean love if it's red or pink, strength and courage for orange or yellow, abundance or healing for green, intuition for blue and purple, protection for black, and clarity for white.

SHELLS

If you live near a body of water, you're more likely to find shells, as they can wash up on shore or be dropped by birds. But they, too, can also be gifts from the spirit world and have a variety of meanings that have transcended time and cultures.

The earliest known picture of a seashell hails from ancient Egypt. And who can forget Sandro Botticelli's

Birth of Venus depicting the goddess rising from the sea in a giant scallop shell? In the nineteenth century, carved shell cameos were extremely popular. (In folklore, cameos carved into shells were thought to bring good health and fortune.) And, of course, pearls, revered by many for eons, come from shellfish.

Shells can be tiny or large, and they provide shelter and sanctuary for many creatures. Seashells are hard and tough, can be used as building materials, and come in all kinds of shapes—from the long, thin mussel to the wide clam and wavy scallop.

All shells represent emotions, due to their association with water, but also strength, resilience, the subconscious, and the journey into the afterlife. Shells can withstand an immense amount of pressure and still retain their power; thus, they signify hope in the face of adversity.

Cowrie shells are considered the voice of the orishas (spirits, forces of nature, or divine power in some West African cultures and gods in the Santeria religion from the Caribbean) and are used for divination. The spirits are telling you something about your future and want you to use a divination tool to assist them. Clams, oysters, scallops, and mussels symbolize femininity and fertility and also beauty and hidden treasures.

If you find a nautilus shell, consider yourself blessed by the spirits. Because these shells have existed for over

500 million years, they signify longevity. The nautilus shell is famous for its spiral structure that follows the golden ratio or Fibonacci sequence. The shape suggests perfection and harmony and also mimics the shape of our galaxy, bringing in cosmic energy and spiritual connection.

STATIC ELECTRICITY

Static electricity can mean getting a little shock when you touch something or your hair standing on end. It can present itself as items sticking to you, or it can even be a tiny arc of bluish light seen only in the dark. It can also be less tangible; you sense it in your body and know it's there, but it has no form. Akin to how it feels before a thunder and lightning storm, there's palpable electricity in the air, and the atmosphere feels dense and alive.

Static electricity tells you that you're in the presence of spirits. Since spirits are energy, sometimes they create a buildup of electrical charge. It is often the very first sign of any spirit activity, and sometimes this is the only sign they have the energy to give. Thus, when you experience static electricity, regardless of the form in which it appears, it means the spirit has been waiting to contact you.

As soon as you feel this sign, it's time to connect. Because there's a buildup of energy, using tools that the spirit must move or electronic devices it can interact with is highly advisable. The spirit may need assistance.

If you feel an electrical charge in the air, the spirit is present and is ready to talk when you are; but if you get an electric shock when you touch something, then it's more urgent. If you're unsure how to get more concrete answers, start with a binary system of yes and no questions and use tools like dowsing rods or a pendulum. If your hair stands on end, spirits could be trying to give you a warning, so be present and mindful. If objects stick to you, they may be telling you it's time to let things (or ideas or negative energy) go.

TEMPERATURE CHANGES ⚡

Maybe you're on a ghost hunt or exploring some old building when you walk through a cold spot. Before assuming a paranormal presence, check for any signs of cold air in the material world. Is there an open window nearby? Is the AC on, or is there a vent near the cold area or a crack in a wall or floor? Once you've determined there's nothing in the physical realm causing the cold spot, you can start thinking about a spirit presence.

Does the cold spot move with you, or does it stay in one place? Can you measure it with a thermometer? I've done paranormal investigations and felt a cold spot. A team member pulled out their portable digital thermometer, and we watched as the numbers dropped drastically in one location with no logical explanation.

The assumption is that spirits, being energy, must draw upon the ambient thermal energy in a room to effect change, leaving some areas cold. So if you feel a cold spot or any other temperature changes that defy reason, you could be experiencing a spirit's presence.

Temperature changes are a general sign of a spirit attempting to get your attention. They've probably been lingering in that area and using up as much energy as they can to do something in the material world that someone will notice. Often when you feel a cold spot, you'll also experience other signs simultaneously, like electrical disturbances or apparitions. You can also test to make sure they're sentient spirits and not merely leftover energy (or lack thereof) by asking them to actively change the temperature while you're using a thermometer or thermal camera. If they respond, you're dealing with a spirit. If not, it may simply be residual energy from recent spiritual activity.

TREES

A tree I didn't plant started growing in my yard. I had a strange feeling that I should leave it alone. Two years later, it was filled with white mulberries. My neighbor was elated. She hadn't seen a white mulberry tree growing wild since she left her home country. I knew then it was a sign for her from her ancestors or someone from her "family tree." Not only are trees signs from spirits, but so is anything they drop in your path—fruit, acorns, leaves, or pine cones.

Trees have been connected to spirituality for ages. Some Wiccan-based practices use the nine sacred woods in ritual bonfires. These woods are the first nine trees in the Celtic tree calendar (which is based on the idea that letters in the ancient Celtic Ogham alphabet are associated with trees).

An alder tree can mean change is coming. If you see an ash tree, pay attention to your dreams for the answers you seek. Birch means rebirth, and hawthorn tells you it's time to decide. A hazel tree provides wisdom, and both holly and rowan offer protection. An oak sends strength and a willow healing.

If an acorn falls in your path, prepare for growth. If you find a heart-shaped leaf, a spirit is sending you love and comfort. An apple could be a message about your health, education, or spirituality. Berries remind you to enjoy the sweetness of life. A peach could be sending love or happiness your way. In Italy, a lemon symbolizes protection, so if one drops near you, pick it up and bring it home to ward off any negative energy. A pine cone is highly spiritual and represents enlightenment and intuition but also perfection and harmony. Like the nautilus, it fans out in the golden ratio or Fibonacci sequence. It also looks like the pineal gland, which many believe is our third eye.

WAVES

Waves can be a powerful message. Many years ago, I went racing down the beach in Malibu hoping to body surf. But when I got in the water, I was sad to find it was very calm—no waves as far as the eye could see. I yelled out loud to all the spirits present to send a sign in a mighty wave, and the next thing I knew, I was swept upside down tumbling in a massive wave. Eventually, the ocean spat me back out on the beach, and I couldn't stop laughing. The lesson I learned was to be careful what you wish for!

Waves, being water, represent emotions, but they have many other meanings as well. If the wave is huge, it can indicate something that will make a big impact in your life. If the waves are small and rippling, this can be a reminder that every action has a ripple effect, whether good or bad. If there are lots of waves, especially ones crashing into one another from different directions, this may be a warning that either you or someone close to you is "making waves" or causing problems. If the weather is stormy and the waves are rough, it can mean trouble ahead, so prepare yourself. If the water is calm, there's smooth sailing ahead, and your journey or future will be peaceful and hassle-free. If the water swirls around in a tidal pool, make sure you aren't spinning yourself in circles.

If the waves are very clear, any answers you seek should clear up soon, or you already know the answer and the spirit is validating you. If the water is muddy or there's fog, there's still confusion around whatever you're asking. Try asking in a different way.

WIND ⁌

The wind is one of the most common signs sent by spirits. It seems they can easily manipulate air currents, so it's often one of the first signs you'll experience, especially if you spend a lot of time in nature or your loved one was a pet.

Pets love to make the wind dance around us! You might step outside on a calm day, ask for a sign, and then see a small fluttering of leaves or maybe feel a slight breeze swirl around you. A blast of air might push you forward, backward, or to the side. The wind might pick up so much that it blows a tree branch down, blocking your path, or foretell a big storm like a tornado or a hurricane. Or you might feel caught up in a whirlwind.

All signs of wind are in the province of intellect, making decisions, and intention. A strong wind is pushing you either toward or away from something or someone. A breeze is a little hello from the afterlife. If it swirls around you, a spirit is sending you comfort and support. If something is blown onto your path, blocking your way, it's a sign that you should stop and reassess. If the wind turns into a bigger storm, it is time not only to physically take shelter but also to take stock of what you've already accomplished before determining what steps you need to take to tackle your next dream.

If you're caught in a whirlwind, that may be pointing to mental confusion and not knowing which way to go or what to do. As a sign, the spirits are saying slow down and stop for a moment. Take a deep breath and listen to your intuition. You already know deep in your heart exactly what you want.

Chapter 5

ANIMALS

When I moved into my house, the yard had no wild-
life. I planted trees and flowers to invite them,
but none appeared. So I left offerings of (vegan) milk and
honey on a table in the backyard and invited spirits to
join me. The next day my yard was filled with small white
butterflies, and they've stayed ever since.

Animals are natural carriers of spirit energy. In some
circles, they're called familiars and have special bonds with
individual people. Some believe that these familiars are
spirit guides or other spiritual allies that are the spirits of
the animals themselves or simply ride them and are drawn
to the person to help them on their life's journey. Some
animals are psychopomps whose job is to guide the spirits
to the other side and carry messages back and forth.

Animals—on land, sea, and air—are often viewed
as signs from the afterlife, especially after you've asked
for a message from a loved one or pet. As with most
signs, they can present in various ways, such as a calm
or agitated cat, and their appearance can have multiple
interpretations. Use your discernment to find the one
that seems to fit best.

BEES ⚜

In 1858, John Greenleaf Whittier, an American Quaker
poet, published a poem called "Telling the Bees." He
wrote about a tradition of telling bees about major life
events, such as deaths (especially if it was the beekeeper),
marriages, and births, so the bees could share in the
event. Otherwise, the bees might stop producing honey
or even die. This tradition might have been inspired by an
old folk belief of Celtic origin, where the bee represents
the spirit of the recently deceased leaving the body.

Bees can appear singularly or in swarms. They can be
angry or buzz happily nearby, bothering nobody. Some
will sting you if they feel threatened. They might be honeybees, bumblebees, or carpenter bees. Honeybees and
bumblebees live in hives, but carpenter bees are solitary.
All bees are pollinators, but only a tiny percentage of bees
make honey.

Typically, if you see a bee after someone has passed,
it means their spirit is visiting you, but the message
depends on the type of bee and how it's acting. If the bee
stings you, it could be a warning but might also represent
overcoming pain, hurt, or betrayal. If the bee is hovering
near you, it's most likely a spirit bringing you a positive
message. Since most bees have hives, the message could
be that you'll find the community you're seeking or that

you're supported by a community of spirits on the other side, especially if the bees are in a swarm.

If you see a honeybee, the spirit is sending you something sweet. Spirits use bumblebees to bring joy and soften any woes. Carpenter bees travel solo, so spirits are telling you that it may be time to pave your own path or to take time out from all your worries. If the bees are covered in pollen, the spirits are bringing good fortune or treasures your way. Or they could be telling you that it's time to stop carrying your burdens and enjoy life.

BUTTERFLIES AND MOTHS ⁂

A beloved pet of mine passed away while I was writing this book. I could hear him, but I second-guessed myself, thinking it was my mind playing tricks to comfort me. I asked for a sign, but nothing seemed to happen. No rainbows or hummingbirds. However, I did notice that my security camera kept notifying me there was an animal in my backyard. Yet every time I checked, there weren't any. I took a closer look and saw clouds of tiny white butterflies. I get visits from them all the time, but they had never set off the motion sensor before. Then it dawned on me—this was the sign from Alexander, my precious cat, telling me he's here and he's okay.

Spirits send butterflies as a sign of transformation and rebirth because they experience metamorphosis—changing from caterpillars to beautiful winged creatures. The spirits are telling you that even though you may be going through changes, don't worry because everything will work out in the end. Growth is necessary for you to become who you're meant to be, and the spirits have your back.

Depending on what colors the butterflies are, the spirits can be sending even more messages. White butterflies often signify simply that the spirits are present and supporting you. If you see a bright orange monarch, it may be time to tap into your creative side and start something new. Yellow butterflies bring joy and happiness, green ones bring love and healing, and blue ones are spirits saying it's time to communicate something you've been holding back. Spirits will send purple butterflies to remind you to listen to your intuition, red to invigorate you, and black to protect you.

All butterflies are sent to remind you of all the beauty in the world, and moths remind you that there's a light in the darkness.

CATS ⁘

Cats exist half in this world and half beyond the veil, so they're natural choices for spirits to use as signs. How the cat acts and their color can suggest the message. So if you ask for a sign and a cat crosses your path (or you see one), pay attention to whether it's mewing or howling at you, rubbing against you, hissing, pouncing, or sleeping and whether it's scrawny or healthy.

All cats represent curiosity and independence, so any cat a spirit sends your way means you should continue searching for the answers you seek and assert your independence and confidence, especially if you're in a job, relationship, or situation that makes you feel insecure or mistreated.

A mewing cat is a spirit reminding you to listen, and a howling one sends caution. If the cat rubs against you flirtatiously and purrs, the spirit is sending you love and, possibly, romance, but if the cat is agitated, hissing, scratching, or twitching its tail, the spirit is warning you that someone around you is not trustworthy and might be gossiping. If the cat is pouncing, the spirit is telling you now is the time to go after your dreams, but if the cat is sleeping, it's time to take a break and recharge. If the cat is scrawny, it's time to scrimp and save, but if the cat is healthy, the spirit is sending you good fortune.

With black cats, the spirits are sending you protection, and with white cats, they are sending guidance and support. Orange cats bring creativity, inspiration, and joy from the spirit realm, while torties and calicos urge you to stand tall and be your authentic self. Gray cats remind you that the world isn't black and white, while tuxedo cats tell you to embrace your duality. Spirits send you strength through tabby cats.

CROWS AND RAVENS ❖

A flock of crows is called a murder, and a group of ravens is an unkindness or conspiracy. They're both predators and scavengers, so ancient people noticed that when they circle overhead, death is near; as a result, they were associated with bad omens. But when a spirit sends you either as a sign, the intentions are rarely bad.

Odin, the Norse god, had two ravens, Huginn and Muninn, who would fly over the lands and report back to him anything they witnessed. Growing up, my grandmother used to say that we had to pay crows respect because they carried the dead to the other side and brought messages from spirits.

Crows and ravens are corvids, which are some of the smartest birds on the planet. So when one appears to you as a sign, the first thing the spirit is telling you is to trust your intellect and rely on your own wisdom and experience. You have everything you need. Use your cunning and intelligence to overcome any obstacle.

If the crows or ravens hang around your yard for a while, consider yourself protected and watched by spirits. If they caw a lot at you, the spirit is saying you should quiet your mind and listen not only to your intuition but also to any mediumship messages that may pop into your mind.

If they're circling overhead, use caution. Someone around you may not have your best interests at heart. Ask the crows or ravens to find out more information for you. Pay attention to your dreams and claircognizant messages to help you figure out whom you need to be wary of.

If two ravens or crows fly overhead together, caw at you, or land near you, the spirits are sending you a partner and companionship, either romantic or platonic.

DOGS, WOLVES, AND COYOTES

Since dog sightings can be a common occurrence in most neighborhoods, make sure to consider the timing of a dog sign. For example, did you spot the dog immediately after asking for a sign or thinking of a deceased person or pet? If yes, it's more likely a sign from the afterlife.

Dogs, like cats, have a general meaning that can also go deeper when you consider the dog's size, color, and actions. Variations to pay attention to are chasing or attacking; snarling or barking; playing loose or on a leash; adult or puppy; big or small; scrawny or healthy; and dog, coyote, or wolf.

Dogs in general represent loyalty, guidance, or companionship offered by spirits. If the dog is chasing something, the spirit is telling you to keep going after your dreams, but if the dog is on the attack, it's time to stop and reassess the situation. Spirits will send a snarling dog as a caution and a barking dog to tell you to pay attention and listen. A dog playing sends messages of hope from the spirit realm, while a dog on a leash warns that you're holding yourself back.

If the dog is a puppy, the spirit is reminding you to tap into your inner child. If the dog is small, whatever you're worried about isn't as bad as you think, and if it's big, something important is on the horizon. If the dog is scrawny, it's time to batten down the hatches, but if it's healthy, spirits are sending you treasure. The type of dog can also be a message, so look into any associated characteristics of different breeds.

If, instead of a dog, you see a coyote, there's trickery afoot. However, if you spot a wolf, you're on the right path.

DOLPHINS AND SEALS ⊹

Maybe you're on vacation or live near a body of water. You ask for a sign from a loved one, look out over the rippling water, and spy a dolphin or seal. Consider yourself lucky because dolphins and seals are powerfully magical signs from spirits. You might catch just a quick glimpse of their head or dorsal fin poking out, or they might dive and splash in the water. They might also appear in groups.

These sea creatures represent emotion, playfulness, intelligence, friendship, and duality. Dolphins are both sea dwellers and mammals, and seals live both on land and in the sea, so when a spirit sends you a sign of either of these magnificent creatures, they are reminding you of your duality. Embrace both sides of your nature. You don't have to be positive all the time. It's okay to be sad and miss someone sometimes, but you should also hold on to the fond memories you had with them.

If the dolphin or seal is acting playful, the spirit is telling you to not take life so seriously all the time. Lighten up and remember to laugh. Connect with your inner child and do something that brings you joy.

If you see a pod of dolphins or seals, spirits are sending you friendship, community, or support. Remain open-minded and seek out group adventures or experiences. You will find your people.

Spirits also send dolphins and seals to help steer you in the right direction. Tell them your troubles and let them help you. These sea creature signs remind you that everything happens for a reason. Any sightings of either dolphins or seals are messages from spirits that you're surrounded by magic. Now is the time to step into your power. Don't be afraid to shine.

DOVES ✣

As far back as the Bible, doves have represented peace, harmony, and hope, but depending on a few factors, they can have other meanings as well. If you see a dove, spirits are telling you that it's time to reconnect with loved ones and pets on the other side. They're waiting to talk with you. They want you to forgive yourself or others, sit still in quiet meditation, and be ready to receive any messages from the spirit realm.

If two turtle doves or mourning doves appear after you've asked for a sign, the spirit is either reminding you how much they loved you or foretelling a new love coming into your life. If the doves are in a flock, there's a journey or adventure on your horizon. If the dove is white, spirits are sending you peace, especially if you've been hurt or sad for a while. If the dove is also cooing, the spirit is soothing you. All they really want is for you to be content and strive for harmony in your life. Any sign of a dove from spirits is telling you there's hope.

FOXES ✣

Foxes have a variety of associations, so when a spirit sends one as a sign, it's important to consider exactly what kind of message you were asking for and the circumstances in which you saw the fox.

Foxes are sneaky but also smart. They can be playing, hunting, or hiding. The most common idiom about them is "cunning as a fox," so spirits are telling you that it's time to trust your own intelligence and common sense. Go with your first instincts and don't second-guess yourself. Deep down, you know exactly what's best for you. Don't let anyone else influence you.

Foxes are also tricksters, so when you see a fox and it appears to be sneaking by, the spirit may be telling you that someone in your midst can't be trusted. Use caution and be alert.

If the fox is hiding, the spirits are telling you to disappear or hide in plain sight until it's safe and you're ready to shine. Use your wisdom to know when is best.

If the fox is playing or carrying something in its mouth, the spirits are sending you an opportunity, so be prepared and pay attention. It will most likely require thinking on your feet.

FROGS AND TOADS ÷

Frogs tend to hop, whereas toads crawl. Frogs are smoother and have a slimy texture, while toads are bumpy and dry. Most frogs and toads start out as tadpoles, so, much like the butterfly, they represent transformation and rebirth. Whether it's a tadpole or adult frog or toad can affect the meaning, as well as if it's croaking, discovered on land or in a pond, and moving toward you or away.

Spotting a frog after asking for a sign is a reminder from a spirit to love every part of yourself, even the parts that repulse you. In other words, turn your frog into a prince with a kiss.

If the frog is hopping, the spirit is telling you to take a leap of faith and start that new project you've been putting off or jump on an opportunity. But if you see a toad crawling or simply sitting, the spirit is telling you to wait.

If you see a tadpole as a sign, be ready for a powerful transformation in your future. Things may seem grim, but the spirit world is supporting you.

Frogs and toads both represent grounded emotions, so spirits send them as signs when they need to remind you not to get swept away by your feelings. If it's a frog, it means the situation is slippery, so use caution. If it's a toad, the road could be bumpy, but it's still worth it.

If either is on land, spirits are telling you to stand firm, but if in a pond, the message is to be fluid and adaptable. If either is moving toward you, an opportunity is coming your way. If they're moving away, you may need to chase your dreams for a bit; but don't worry, spirits will help you catch up.

HUMMINGBIRDS ⚘

In my personal experience, hummingbirds are the most common animal sign from the afterlife. Nearly every time I've asked for a message, especially from a pet, I've seen one. After a cat I was hoping to rescue died, I went outside and asked for a sign. A hummingbird not only appeared but flew so low around my head that I could hear and feel its tiny wings fluttering.

Hummingbirds move their wings in the shape of an infinity symbol, connecting them to eternity. As such, they're considered messengers of the spirit realm. You might see them flying or hovering and hear the steady beat of their tiny wings. These fast wings symbolize quick thinking, so the spirit is telling you to trust your first impressions and go with your gut.

If the hummingbird circles your head, you're surrounded by spirit energy that you can tap into anytime for guidance and help. Tell the little bird what you need.

If you're experiencing relationship issues, spirits will send a hummingbird as a symbol of love and to remind you to keep your heart open, especially if the bird is red or green. They're very brave as well, so when spirits send them as a sign, they're telling you to be strong and courageous in the face of adversity.

If the bird is moving backward, they're reminding you to hold on to precious memories of deceased loved ones and pets and to seek answers in the past. However, if they're drinking from a flower when you ask for a sign, spirits are reminding you to be here in the present and not overwhelm yourself. Instead, focus on what's right in front of you, on the first step, or on what you can accomplish now. You have all you need.

LADYBUGS ⁙

Does your local plant nursery or hardware store sell live ladybugs? Well, that's because they eat the pests that damage plants and crops. As a result, they're a symbol of good luck and protection.

Ladybugs are named after the Virgin Mary. Legend has it that sometime during the Middle Ages, crops were decimated by pests, so the villagers prayed to Mary. A swarm of bugs appeared and saved the harvest. They named them Our Lady's Beetle, which, over time, became ladybug. So if you ask for a sign and spirits send you a ladybug, they're sending you good fortune and a shield of protection.

If the ladybug lands on you, make a wish. A spirit is with you and will carry your wish to the other side, and it will manifest in the real world.

If you spot a swarm of ladybugs, the spirits are gathering to send you many treasures and opportunities as well as either a new or expanded community. Expect good tidings, but don't forget to keep working hard and striving. Spirits help you best if you're already working toward a goal instead of sitting around and waiting for an opportunity.

Ladybugs can come in different colors, which adds to the spiritual message. If the bugs are the more common red with black dots, spirits are primarily sending you luck. But if they're black with red dots, the focus is on protection. Yellow ladybugs with black dots are the spirits sending you joy and happiness, and if the ladybugs are more orange, expect some creative inspiration from the spirit realm.

Whatever you do, if you see a ladybug, don't kill it. Killing a ladybug is considered very bad luck. If you kill one by accident, ask the spirits for forgiveness.

OWLS

Owls have been synonymous with wisdom for eons due to their keen senses. The ancient Greeks associated owls with Athena, the goddess of wisdom, because Athens was full of little owls who kept watch from high perches all over the city, much like the deities—especially Athena, their patron.

Owls, like crows, are closely associated with spirits and were considered guides of the dead in ancient cultures. The ancient Greeks also linked the nocturnal owls with the moon and associated their night vision with psychic insight and prophecy.

Since owls see in the dark, spirits send you one as a sign when it's time to do shadow work and tap into your subconscious. Ask yourself if you're reacting instead of being in the moment and what past trauma could have caused that reaction. Embrace the trauma, process it, and let it go. It no longer serves you. Then allow yourself to simply be present when confronted with conflict or adversity so you can deal with the situation by tapping into your wisdom instead of your emotions.

If you can see the owl, the spirits are sending you sharp vision and guiding you to clearly see anything that's been hidden. If you hear the owl but can't see it, the spirits are warning you of something on the horizon. Keep your eyes and ears open and remain calm. When you're prepared, you can handle any situation.

If the owl is white, spirits are telling you that you already know what you must do. Stop procrastinating and begin. If the owl tilts its head, the spirit is confused by your question or request and wants you to reconsider your words or desires.

All owl sightings tell you to use your intuition and inner wisdom.

RABBITS AND HARES ⁘

The Greek goddess of hunting, Artemis, would not allow hares to be harmed. Across all cultures and traditions, rabbits and hares symbolize the same thing—good luck (as in the rabbit's foot charm), fertility, abundance, rebirth, and vulnerability. How the rabbit or hare acts or looks when you see one after asking for a sign affects the message, but the core meaning is the same: When spirits send you a sign in the form of a rabbit or hare, they're sending you prosperity and luck. If you asked if you'd have children, a family, success, or wealth and spirits send you a rabbit or hare, the answer is yes.

If the rabbit or hare is hopping when you spot them, the spirit is gently nudging you to "hop to it" and get started on whatever you've been putting off. If you've been wondering about moving or traveling, a hopping bunny tells you to get ready to hop around.

If the rabbit or hare hides or if you also spot a rabbit hole, spirits are telling you to be vulnerable, take risks, and step out of your comfort zone. It will be worth it once you realize you can make all your dreams come true. They also remind you that it's okay if you don't have all the answers right now. Everything will be revealed in time, but you must take the first step before any doors will open.

White rabbits are a sign of purity and innocence, so spirits are telling you to be your authentic self. If they send a black rabbit, make sure you know who your real friends are before you share your dreams and goals.

SNAKES ⚬⚬

In the Bible, a snake (or serpent) tempted Eve to eat fruit of the tree of knowledge. In Hebrew, the word for snake is linked to divination. Kundalini, in Sanskrit, is coiled, snakelike energy that rests at the base of the spine and unfurls to reach up through the body and connect with the spirit realm. In ancient Egypt and Mesopotamia, snakes represented eternal life. The ancient Greek god of medicine, Asclepius, was often associated with a snake wrapped around a rod or branch of the tree of life, a symbol still used today.

If a spirit sends you a snake in the grass, someone around you isn't trustworthy. If you know the snake is poisonous, someone close to you is venomous and gossiping. If the snake blocks your path, you're going about things the wrong way. Use your cunning to get around the obstacle.

A lot of people are afraid of snakes, so they also represent fear. If the spirits send you a snake as a sign, they're telling you to not let fear stop you from fulfilling your goals.

If you find a snakeskin or see a snake shedding its skin, spirits are saying either you're going through a transition or you need to shed your own skin and allow yourself to transform.

If the snake is coiled like an ouroboros (an ancient symbol showing a serpent or dragon eating its own tail), the spirits are warning you not to hide your vulnerability. Instead, show your authentic self to the world. You'll attract the right people and opportunities. They're also reminding you of the cyclical nature of life. Everything has its time, comes to an end, and is reborn. Trust the process.

If the snake is in a tree, be ready to receive good health.

SPIDERS

Aside from their eight legs, spiders are known for their webs. Weaving and webs are tied to many attributes, from weaving your own destiny to the World Wide Web and communication. If you ask for a sign and see a spider, take note of its size, what it's doing, its color or type, and whether it has prey. Typically, spiders represent good luck, fate, connection, and warnings.

If you see a spider weaving a web, the spirit world is aligning opportunities to help you fulfill your life's purpose and achieve your desires. Don't give up!

If the spider is hanging out in the web alert and ready but has no prey yet, the spirits are about to send you some inspiration, so get ready to channel them and start any creative projects you've been putting off or planning.

If there's a bug stuck in the web, the spirits know you're having trouble manifesting your dreams. More action is required on your part before they can help. Clearly state out loud to the spirits exactly what your intentions are. If you've already done that and still feel stuck, it means you need to take the first step to put you in a better position for any spirits to assist you.

If you find webs in your house, the spirits are sending you good fortune, but if you spot an abandoned web, the spirits are telling you it's time to let go of anything that no longer serves you.

If you see many little spiders or one big one, the spirits are sending you prosperity. If they're gold or brown, they're sending you success. Black widow spiders are a warning that someone close to you can't be trusted.

Track Your Signs from the Afterlife

DATE: _____

TIME: _____

YOUR SIGN: _____

YOUR MESSAGE: _____

_____

_____

_____

_____

DATE: _____

TIME: _____

YOUR SIGN: _____

YOUR MESSAGE: _____

_____

_____

_____

_____

DATE:

TIME:

YOUR SIGN:

YOUR MESSAGE:

DATE:

TIME:

YOUR SIGN:

YOUR MESSAGE:

30 Real Signs from the Afterlife

DATE: _____

TIME: _____

YOUR SIGN: _____

YOUR MESSAGE: _____

_____

_____

_____

_____

_____

DATE: _____

TIME: _____

YOUR SIGN: _____

YOUR MESSAGE: _____

_____

_____

_____

_____

_____

DATE:

TIME:

YOUR SIGN:

YOUR MESSAGE:

DATE:

TIME:

YOUR SIGN:

YOUR MESSAGE:

DATE:

TIME:

YOUR SIGN:

YOUR MESSAGE:

DATE:

TIME:

YOUR SIGN:

YOUR MESSAGE:

DATE: _____

TIME: _____

YOUR SIGN: _____

YOUR MESSAGE: _____

_____

_____

_____

_____

DATE: _____

TIME: _____

YOUR SIGN: _____

YOUR MESSAGE: _____

_____

_____

_____

_____

_____

30 Real Signs from the Afterlife

DATE:

TIME:

YOUR SIGN:

YOUR MESSAGE:

DATE:

TIME:

YOUR SIGN:

YOUR MESSAGE:

DATE:

TIME:

YOUR SIGN:

YOUR MESSAGE:

DATE:

TIME:

YOUR SIGN:

YOUR MESSAGE:

DATE:

TIME:

YOUR SIGN:

YOUR MESSAGE:

DATE:

TIME:

YOUR SIGN:

YOUR MESSAGE:

DATE:

TIME:

YOUR SIGN:

YOUR MESSAGE:

DATE:

TIME:

YOUR SIGN:

YOUR MESSAGE:

DATE:

TIME:

YOUR SIGN:

YOUR MESSAGE:

DATE:

TIME:

YOUR SIGN:

YOUR MESSAGE:

RESOURCES

Branden Lyesmith

brandentarot.com

Branden is the psychic-medium I call on when I need a little extra help. You can book him through his website.

The Dark Zone Network

thedarkzone.tv

This network gave me my biggest break: a live-streaming paranormal investigation at the Los Angeles Police Department Museum on the episode titled "Haunted Hollywood: Inside LAPD Station #11." It streams many live ghost hunts on its app and website.

Dead Air: Full Spectrum with Ken and George

youtube.com/c/DeadAirFullSpectrum

This is one of my favorite paranormal shows to be on, guest cohost, and watch.

The Green Man

thegreenmanstore.com

The store where I give readings in North Hollywood, California, is an amazing resource for everything related to spirits.

Karen Rontowski

karenrontowski.com

Karen is as funny as she is gifted. I thoroughly enjoyed being on her informative podcast *Paranormal Karen*, which you can find on her website.

Renée Watt

rainbowglitterstar.com

Renée was the first person to encourage me to give public readings and is an excellent reader herself.

Sheena Metal

sheenametalspiritual.com

Sheena was the first person to interview me live. She's a phenomenal host with tons of paranormal experience.

Wine, Spirits, and Witches

winespiritsandwitches.com

This podcast with Monica and Shana is perfect for beginners and all levels of witches, psychics, and ghost-curious folks.

Dvn8

rightalignment.co/dvn8

This free app uses sophisticated technology to connect your intuition to the wisdom of ancient archetypes, and the results are scarily accurate.

Ghosts Believe in Me: Playing Monsters by Day, Seeking Spirits at Night by Rick McCallum

I met Rick McCallum while ghost hunting, and we became fast friends. He gave me a copy of his book, and it's a must-read.

REFERENCES

Andrews, Ted. *How to Do Psychic Readings through Touch*. Woodbury, MN: Llewellyn Publications, 2018.

Barnum, Melanie. *The Book of Psychic Symbols: Interpreting Intuitive Messages*. Woodbury, MN: Llewellyn Publications, 2021.

Buckland, Raymond. *Signs, Symbols & Omens: An Illustrated Guide to Magical & Spiritual Symbolism*. Woodbury, MN: Llewellyn Publications, 2020.

Crisp, Tony. *Dream Dictionary: An A to Z Guide to Understanding Your Unconscious Mind*. New York: Dell, 2002.

DeBord, J. M. *The Dream Interpretation Dictionary: Symbols, Signs, and Meanings*. Canton, MI: Visible Ink Press, 2017.

Goldberg, Eili. *The Ultimate Dictionary of Dreams*. Hod Hasharon, Israel: Astrolog Publishing House, 1999.

Grant, Richard. "Do Trees Talk to Each Other?" *Smithsonian Magazine*. February 21, 2018. smithsonianmag.com/science-nature/the-whispering-trees-180968084.

Hill, Silvia. *Mediumship: An Essential Guide to Being a Medium, Spirit Channeling, and Spiritual Development*. Silvia Hill, 2022.

Kuzmeskus, Elaine. *The Art of Mediumship*. Atglen, PA: Schiffer Publishing Ltd., 2012.

Kuzmeskus, Elaine. *Séance 101: Physical Mediumship: Table Tipping, Psychic Photography, Trumpet Séances, and Other Important Phenomena*. Atglen, PA: Schiffer Publishing Ltd., 2007.

Mauriello, Joseph J. *Only a Thought Away*. Lincoln, NE: iUniverse, Inc., 2005.

McGillivray, Debbie, and Eve Adamson. *The Complete Idiot's Guide to Pet Psychic Communication*. New York: Alpha, 2004.

Newman, Rich. *Ghost Hunting for Beginners: Everything You Need to Know to Get You Started*. Woodbury, MN: Llewellyn Publications, 2011.

Ragan, Lyn. *Signs from Pets in the Afterlife: Identifying Messages from Pets in Heaven*. Atlanta, GA: Lyn Ragan, 2015.

Rinpoché, Guru. *The Tibetan Book of the Dead*. Translated by Francesca Fremantle and Chogyam Trungpa. Boston: Shambhala Publications, Inc., 2000.

Russo, Kim. *The Happy Medium*. New York: HarperCollins, 2016.

Ryan, George. "Did You Know? Ladybugs Are Named for the Virgin Mary." *UCatholic*. April 24, 2018. ucatholic.com/blog/ did-you-know-ladybugs-are-named-for-the-virgin-mary.

Schwartzberg, Louie, director. *Fantastic Fungi*. Moving Art, 2019. 1 hr., 21 min. netflix.com/title/81183477.

Smith, Gordon. *Intuitive Studies: A Complete Course in Mediumship*. London: Hay House UK, Ltd., 2012.

Stymacks, Amelia. "Why Ravens and Crows Are Earth's Smartest Birds." *National Geographic*. March 19, 2018. nationalgeographic .co.uk/animals/2018/03/why-ravens-and-crows-are-earths -smartest-birds.

Sylvia, Browne. *Contacting Your Spirit Guide*. Carlsbad, CA: Hay House, Inc., 2005.

Todeschi, Kevin J., and Carol Ann Liaros. *Edgar Cayce on Auras & Colors*. Virginia Beach, VA: ARE Press, 2012.

Wasserman, James. *The Egyptian Book of the Dead: The Book of Going Forth by Day*. Translated by Dr. Raymond O. Faulkner. San Francisco: Chronicle Books, 2015.

Wigington, Patti. "What Are the Nine Sacred Woods of a Bonfire?" *Learn Religions*. June 25, 2019. learnreligions.com/sacred -woods-of-the-bonfire-2562763.

Wright, Sara. "Rabbit/Hare Mythology: The Rabbit and the Moon." *Over the Edge and Beyond: Journal of a Naturalist*. March 27, 2018. sarawrightnature.wordpress.com/tag/rabbit-hare-mythology.

INDEX

ACKNOWLEDGMENTS

Thank you to my grandmother, Vera, for teaching me about spirits; my parents and stepparents; Jeremy Graham; Amy Wallace for editing my first book and being an eternal friend; Renee Watt; Rochelle Evans; Karen Rontowski; Kate Morgan; Rory Gory; Sheena Metal; Patti Negri; Stephanie Hyden and Darren Bousman; Susan Slaughter, Jay Bluemke, Rick McCallum, Cheryl, Mikey, Meesha, and everyone at The Dark Zone Network; Griffin, Carrie, Jill, Joe, Branden, Pleasant, and everyone else at The Green Man; *Dead Air*'s Ken and George; Yvette, Natalie, Venus, Catie, Annette, Jacqui, Regina, Celeste, Dylan, Mena, Leah, Charlotte, Annie, Mimi; and all my students, clients, cats, social media friends, and spirit guides.

ABOUT THE AUTHOR

 **Melissa St. Hilaire** grew up in the backwoods of Massachusetts, had her first mediumship experience at age three, began reading tarot cards at twelve, and has been mystified by the occult ever since. An intuitive reader and medium at The Green Man in North Hollywood, California, she offers spellcrafting services, a psychic development series, mediumship training, and Victorian table-tipping séances. Although she read privately for many years, her career launched after she was selected to be one of four psychics for Midsummer Scream's famous Leota's Lounge at the Grim Grinning Gala. Since then, she's been featured in many paranormal podcasts and publications. Visit her website, americanwitch13.com, and follow her on social media: @ americanwitch13 on Instagram, Twitter, and Facebook.